PRAISE FOR THE AUTHOR

"Geraldine is one of the people I will always value knowing, working with and getting to know over a long period of time.

Geraldine has many skills but it is the combination of skill, passion and principle, overlaid with compassion that enables her to deliver outstanding results. I am pleased to see that she has shared her thoughts and experiences with others in this book."

Terry Murphy
Publisher of the Achievement Process
Walton-on-Thames, UK

"A thought-provoking read that demonstrates the challenge, and at times loneliness, of the leadership role. Geraldine's shared thoughts and experiences during a time of extraordinary history and change, show that being true to yourself, those close to you, and those against you, is difficult and confronting, but will ultimately be seen to be the right thing to do. This book shows that Geraldine made a difference and inspires others to do the same."

Sean Jameson
Manager Human Resources
Taxi Services Commission

"You meet people every day that talk about caring about some issue or another, but very rarely do you meet someone who takes action to do something about what they care for. Geraldine is one of those rare people. We would describe Geraldine as courageous, tenacious, curious and authentic. Often there is a personal expense for those individuals who refuse to look away, who don't hesitate to voice the injustice they see. Geraldine has paid personally for what she has confronted – which has made her stronger. Congratulations Geraldine."

Lynn Johnson and Peter Lanius,
Directors of Leadership Mastery Pty Ltd

"If you've ever faced a difficult decision in your life then this book will inspire you. It's a true story of really being tested, having the courage of your convictions and then making a tough decision that would be significantly life changing. Geraldine and her family did all of that and have come out the other side all the better for all they've experienced.

This path has made Geraldine a strong and courageous leader who shows resilience and humility and in so doing, inspires those around her to achieve great things."

Maria Zerella,
Manager Learning and Development, WorkSafe Victoria

"I had the extreme good fortune to work with Geraldine in South Africa during the 1990's. This was a time of immense transition, as the weakening tentacles of the 'old' South Africa fought to retain some meaningful influence in the 'new'. Conflict before and after Mandela's inauguration continued at various levels and across different parts of society.

During this unpredictable time Geraldine was intimately involved in resolving conflict between rival parties. Her conciliation and mediation work was inspiring and often unique.

She worked tirelessly to bring disputing factions together by showing them why compromise made sense and how it could work. At other times her active mind and creative flair lead to 'win-win' outcomes that no one would have believed possible - least of all the combatants.

Her personal power is driven by her unbounded energy and endless enthusiasm. She refuses to be distracted by problems or deterred by obstacles. She works through, over, under and around them. That she has recently committed herself to writing this book at this time makes perfect sense."

Steve Woods.
CEO - The Achievement Network Africa

"In a world where we are all too politically correct, it is refreshing to meet people like Geraldine driven by passion and purpose. She has shown great courage to recount the stories of those who battled for a greater cause than themselves. Leaders are what make this world turn around by their cause, their purpose, their compassion for others. This is what has inspired me personally about Geraldine and her story. Someone needs to tell this powerful and often painful story. I thank Geraldine for having the guts to help many people have closure and for others to learn and be inspired. Inspired by overcomers such as Geraldine and others who took a stand against great adversity for the betterment of us all."

Wayne Dyson, Director, Bridgeworks

"Geraldine Coy, author of 'Brave Truth', will take the reader on a journey of resilience and courage that will show the strength of character needed in overcoming adversity.

This true story powerfully tells of the struggle for post-apartheid freedom and gives insights into the depth of violence and the retributions that came from that.

This book will grip the reader and hold you enthralled with its thought provoking and powerful story. It will inspire and touch your heart, leading you to achieve greater things.

'Brave Truth' is aptly named, as indeed the author is very brave in portraying her incredible life-changing story that will challenge the reader to rise up and overcome adversities faced."

Karen Scott
Author, Speaker, Success Coach

BRAVE TRUTH

Global Publishing Group
Australia • New Zealand • Singapore • America • London

BRAVE TRUTH

POWERFUL UNTOLD STORIES OF THE STRUGGLE FOR POST-APARTHEID FREEDOM.

GERALDINE COY

DISCLAIMER

All the information, techniques, skills and concepts contained within this publication are of the nature of general comment only and are not in any way recommended as individual advice. The intent is to offer a variety of information to provide a wider range of choices now and in the future, recognising that we all have widely diverse circumstances and viewpoints. Should any reader choose to make use of the information contained herein, this is their decision, and the contributors (and their companies), authors and publishers do not assume any responsibilities whatsoever under any condition or circumstances. It is recommended that the reader obtain their own independent advice.

First Edition 2013

National Library of Australia
Cataloguing-in-Publication entry:

Coy, Geraldine, author

Brave Truth: Powerful Untold Stories of the Struggle for Post-Apartheid Freedom / Geraldine Coy.

1st ed.
ISBN: 9781922118264 (paperback)

Post-apartheid era – South Africa.
Apartheid – South Africa.
Human rights – South Africa.
South Africa – Race relations.
South Africa – Politics and government – 20th century.
South Africa – Social conditions – 20th century.

323.119606809

Published by Global Publishing Group
PO Box 517 Mt Evelyn, Victoria 3796 Australia
Email info@TheGlobalPublishingGroup.com

For Further information about orders:
Phone: +61 3 9736 1156 or Fax +61 3 8648 6871

I dedicate this book to the incredibly brave people who, despite the real risk to themselves, took the definitive steps to front up to the Commission Hearings when it was evident that the criminal justice system had failed them. You have demonstrated great courage and hope in your quest to be heard, to be acknowledged, to be understood.
I also dedicate this book to my darling husband Dave and my amazingly resilient children, James, Thomas and Rachel, for supporting me through the resultant upheaval in their lives. You have kept me whole and I love you with all my heart.

Geraldine Coy

ACKNOWLEDGEMENTS

I have so many people to thank for getting me to this point. It is a truly humbling process in trying to ensure that I cover all the wonderful people who have been so much a part of my life, and who have helped me get to this point. I find that I cannot do this justice, and so I have opted for a highly inadequate general statement of thanks. It is meant sincerely, though, with all my heart.

I wish to acknowledge and thank my many friends and colleagues who have contributed to my thinking over the years.

Leonard Cohen's ANTHEM gives me permission to be flawed, when he sings:

"Ring the bells that still can ring
Forget your perfect offering
There is a crack, a crack in everything
That's how the light gets in."

I don't pretend to be anything other than what I am, an unextraordinary person, but I am grateful for the extraordinary life I have been given and mostly for the people with whom I share it. My family, colleagues and friends have loudly debated life with me in countless bottles of wine over hundreds of lunches and dinner parties. They have given me safe haven, cajoled and lectured me, and generally kept me happily assured of my failings. They have also encouraged me and given me permission to be myself.

I thank you all who taught me so much, who shared your knowledge, skills, advice, guidance and love so generously. It is from you that I learned so much of myself as you mirrored the Truth.

FREE BONUS GIFT

**Valued at $97.00 –
But Yours <u>FREE!</u>**

Claim your FREE BONUS GIFT by going to
www.BraveTruthTheBook.com/Bonus

Instant Access and FREE Download

As a way of saying thank you for investing in this book, I'd like to give you a free special audio program "Secrets behind the Truth". This audio bonus explores the reasons why we disguise ourselves daily, as we shy away from disclosure of our True selves.

It's a fascinating look at what drives us to hide behind masks – from school age children to business professionals. We'll share with you the experience of a variety of people who will enable a better understanding of courageous conversations, how to have them and how to make them successful.

"The personal character of Truth arises from the rich tapestry of life. It is out of adversity that great courage is born."

Claim your FREE BONUS GIFT by going to
www.BraveTruthTheBook.com/Bonus

CONTENTS

A FOREWORD NOTE FROM THE AUTHOR

"For to be free is not merely to cast off one's chains, but to live in a way that respects and enhances the freedom of others" Nelson Mandela

I have found that without the mutual obligation of us all to each other, to build a future based on respect for our rights; to live as we choose to live; to have a home which we can call a safe place; and the right to bring our children up in a world where their opportunities will be as broad as their dreams and as real as their efforts, we won't be able to take the next step toward this goal.

I have tried to demonstrate that true compassion is a firm and rational decision made with sound reasoning, and does not falter even in the face of those who behave badly. That does not mean that I have ever shied away from the need for those responsible for bad behaviour to be held accountable in some form or another.

In this book, you will be invited into the truth behind the real cause(s) of violence and the perpetration of terrible acts of retribution within communities driven by despair and poverty. The complexities of these communities, their history forged in the Apartheid regime, the values of their traditional leadership and the emergence of a new local order, thrown into a melting pot of controversy, all prevented the development of anything close to a safe society.

Geraldine Coy

INTRODUCTION

I am proud to be a South African. These are words which must have crossed the lips of millions in our country since the national elections of 1994.

There was never a debate in my mind, although the question had been raised many times before. Would we be leaving the country? We would not. We were going to stay. I had not consciously explored the reasons for this and did not register at the time why I was so strongly committed to this decision. I knew that my whole family would be equally committed and it was a statement made with some pride.

Something Atholl Fugard had said whilst being interviewed on television on the 10th of October, 1993, had resonated strongly with me. He was explaining to Ruda Landman how, when his passport was withdrawn for a period of five years somewhere in the sixties, he was at a stage in his writing career when his plays were achieving acclaim overseas and he was receiving invitations to Manhatttan and Europe. He said that had he not been refused exit, he could so easily have been seduced into another world, another life. He had been forced to focus on what he had left, the people of South Africa and his audiences there. The rest, for the purposes of this book, is unimportant but at the time the flame of nationhood roared strongly in my heart and soul and I was so truly proud to be a part of such significant change.

I had lost so many friends to foreign lands, all quoting their insecurities, fears for their children and all the reasons we know so well. All had left regretfully, expressing a love for their country and a deep resentment for the system which had rendered residence there unbearable. Thoughout challenging debates I had battled to understand but was careful not to indulge in the sanctimonious trap of an emotional judgement on the basis of the so called "chicken run." For many, the decision had been traumatic and I had respect for the integrity with which it had been made.

At the beginning of 1993 some began to return. Why was this? Was this because so many strides had been made at the World Trade Centre where the peaceful transition following democratic elections involving all of South Africa's citizens, for the first time, was being negotiated? Why now, when the country was in its deepest turmoil of pain and violence? Chris Hani had been assassinated on the 10th of April, 1993, leaving the SACP (South African Communist Party), without its political leader. At the time, the SACP and the ANC (African National Congress) were comrades in the push for a new order. The assassination, suspected at the time of being part of the conservative right wing backlash to the negotiations, sparked great fears that this would risk the negotiations themselves and everyone's hopes clung to a negotiated agreement for all. So why were these people returning? It was odd.

Odder still was the generic response. "We are South Africans and we left when we foresaw the problems of the present and the future. In a tragic way, if you mess it up you will have justified our decision to leave. If you don't and now there is hope that you won't, then we'll never have that claim again."

And therein lies the irony. To reclaim their roots with national pride, those who returned and those who stayed, felt the need to be part of the transition. I wonder at the love of the people for this nation and perhaps the true miracle of 1994 lies within our capacity for change. Indeed, I was proud.

The cruelty of the apartheid system had cost all South Africans dearly. It was only at that time that we had the freedom to engage with one another and to begin the healing of prejudices entrenched through separation. We were full of hope that our generation would build the bridges to cross the rivers of fear which had not only carried, but also cemented prejudice in turbulent times.

To quote André Brink, this had indeed been a "Dry White Season," arid and infertile, offering no hope of growth, a world of deprivation and sorrow for us all.

And so I thanked Mr Fugard for his sensitive insights and set my own sights on rebuilding our hope and trust in each other. I thought this a gift, an opportunity to make a difference and to begin a new life together, so much more enriched through our agony. In the next four years there were many moments of truth for me where this decision was reinforced a hundred fold and I exulted in the wins as we stepped our way through truth and learned that we could rise above the natural enmities and hatred which had burned for so long. The Truth and Reconciliation Commission, inspired by Nelson Mandela's belief in forgiveness and driven by the passion, zeal and compassion of Archbishop Desmond Tutu, was a lesson for the world in what an extraordinary nation South Africa had the capacity to be.

Anyone witnessing Nelson Mandela's walk out onto the field at Ellis Park, (the epicentre of Afrikanerdom - built by the notoriously influential Broederbond - apartheid's stamp on nationhood), after South Africa's win against New Zealand in the 1995 Rugby World Cup, would remember the goosebumps and can still feel that awe inspiring recognition of a miracle happening before our eyes. He had chosen "the game of apartheid" to show all South Africans that there was hope to be found in a joint, shared victory under a new flag. He was wearing the number 6 rugby jersey of the Springbok Captain, Francois Pienaar.

The roar of the crowd deafened everyone in the stadium and spectators, who at the start of the game had refused to join in the singing of a joint and multilingual national anthem, found themselves levitating upwards in a standing ovation. It was fantastic! There were tears of joy, respect, love, honour, hope, courage and a national pride I had never felt, nor thought I'd ever see. It had happened and now everyone could see a new pathway forward to that pot of gold at the end of the rainbow.

The dancing in the streets of downtown Johannesburg, the joyous bouncing of cars, the jiving on corners, the entangling of white and black arms as we flouted all the road rules to spontaneously create one of the biggest parties ever was so wonderfully rich for us all. Indeed, this was the birth of the rainbow nation. On that day at least, all the naysayers were silenced and we were all so proud.

All this came to an abrupt and traumatic end for me on the 10th of December, 1998.

Green and gold president

JUNE 26,1995: during the build-up to the Rugby World Cup, Mandela comes out in support of retaining the controversial Springbok emblem.

Soon afterwards, in one of his most evocative nation-building gestures, Madiba dons the Number Six jersey and takes the Rugby World Cup winners' podium at Ellis Park with Springbok captain Francois Pienaar.

July 19, 1995: Mandela signs the Truth Commission legislation into being, warning "South Africans everywhere" to prepare themselves for participation in the process.

July, 1995: At a lunch at his official Pretoria residence, he brings together the widows and wives of the country's apartheid leaders and those of veteran leaders of the liberation movement.

November 29, 1995: Mandela names Archbishop Desmond Tutu as head of the 17-member Truth Commission.

Mandela meets with former president PW Botha in the first of a series of failed attempts to get him to testify to the Truth and Reconciliation Commission — and to brief him on the decision to charge former defence minister General Magnus Malan, and 10 other top Botha-era military veterans, in connection with the murder of 13 people in KwaZulu-Natal in 1987.

CAPPING THE GLORY: Mandela congratulates victorious Bok skipper Francois Pienaar.

March 1996: Madiba takes a series of heart and blood tests to allay rumours about his health to steady a shaky rand. He makes another inspirational sports appearance, this time for Bafana Bafana before their Africa Cup of Nations victory, striding onto the field wearing a soccer shirt.

May 9, 1996: Mandela "expresses regret" at the NP's decision to pull out of the Government of National Unity, saying it will benefit "neither them nor the ANC".

July 1996: Madiba visits the United Kingdom on an official visit, wowing the British and spending some time hosted by Queen Elizabeth and the Duke of Edinburgh, before visiting Paris where his tour is an even greater success.

July 18, 1996: On his 78th birthday, he is serenaded by the "King of Pop" Michael Jackson who was in South Africa on a tour.

December 10, 1996: Mandela signs into law South Africa's new Constitution, hailed as one of the most democratic in the world — finally consigning apartheid to the legal scrapheap.

CHAPTER 1

A LESSON IN SOCIAL ENGINEERING

Chapter 1

A LESSON IN SOCIAL ENGINEERING

This will be a difficult read. By their very nature, the facts of the origins of conflict are buried deep in history and the prior life experiences of the main characters. I have attempted to position these allegiances as accurately as possible and it should be remembered that much is based on the lens through which I, as an outsider to these stories, a white woman from a privileged community, was allowed to look.

Thus, the reader should not try at first glance to completely understand all the nuances of these facts. I place them in front of you purely to reinforce the view that this is indeed a complicated web of hardly understandable proportions. However, there is a thread of logic to it which, at the end of the day, makes a bizarre sense of what happened. And so I ask you to trust me.

It's the early 1980s. The migration of black people from the homelands * and the independent Transkei Republic had, since the mid 1970s, taken place at an accelerated rate and the authorities had been unprepared for the influx.

The apartheid laws of the time made migrants from the homelands, "illegal immigrants." These people, struggling to find work to feed their families, were at the time, prior to the Wiehahn Commission's 1980 legislative change* not given the status of "employee" in the working world. This had effectively rendered them powerless to organise any collective argument against the state.

The regime's batons of power had been suppression, repression and oppression in the form of the emergency regulations, allowing for the arrest and detention of individuals for a period of at least three months without trial. Known "activists" were "banned" in their own country and any collective of more than two people at any time was considered a "crowd" determined to undermine the State. Arrests, followed frequently by disappearances, were regular occurrences.

In the Western Cape, prior to the early 1980s, no new land had been made available for black settlement outside the homelands for nearly thirteen years. Ninety nine year leaseholds had not been made available to black people, with preference being given to other race groups - white, coloured, Malay and Indian - more settled in the Western Cape at that time. Labour laws at the time reinforced these preferences.

Illegal immigrants settled in Crossroads, erecting the only homes they could build from wood, corrugated iron sheets and plastic, materials often gleaned from rubbish dump sites.

Some time in early 1980, Pik Botha, Minister of Foreign Affairs serving under State President P.W. Botha, had made the connection between domestic policy and foreign affairs. He would have understood the threat to South Africa's economy from further sanctions and sought to develop the country's internal capacity. He was therefore known as a "verligte," or an "enlightened" politician. The story goes that he took a helicopter flight and that with him, allegedly, was the Minister of Co-operation and Development, Dr. Piet Koornhof. It is true that this flight would have taken place on a great day in Cape Town (for it would not have been safe to fly in any other conditions) and I can see the magnificence of Table Mountain receding behind them. In front, the stunning walled terraces of the University of Cape Town overlooked by the Cecil John Rhodes Memorial and the huge lions which guard it and to the right, the world renowned gardens of Kirstenbosch. Having flown over the wealthy suburbs of Newlands and Rondebosch making their way towards the N2 Highway, the scenery would begin to be tarnished by the dirty markings of the squatter communities in shanty towns.

Above the thump-thump of the helicopter's revolutionary blades, Pik was explaining to Piet the need for more labour to be brought into the increasingly industrialised areas of Cape Town. The growth in the current labour market wasn't fast enough to cope with increased demand in the manufacturing industries and cheap labour was needed. Looking down on the area between Nyanga and Gugulethu there was a relatively open space. But how to manage the influx? This would have been Piet's concern. With Pik's persuasive support, Piet was set to "negotiate an agreement" with the assistance of the Urban Foundation and other locally active organisations.

And so it came about that the Koornhof Agreement allowed the residents of Crossroads to be properly enumerated and that those who wanted to stay and who qualified in terms of certain criteria (which we'll explore later) would be granted temporary rights under Section 10 (1) (d) of the legislation* and the plan was to develop housing for them. Only part of what became known as New Crossroads was ever developed because, as I said, the influx was not managed quite according to plan.

The plan was that the existing Crossroads community would assist with the enumeration. If these illegal immigrants could be counted then they would qualify for temporary rights and then they could get work and avoid detention without their "pass."* Even more attractive, they would qualify for a house.

Under the benevolent appointment of the apartheid government, two leaders were recognised in Crossroads at the time. Johnson

Ngxobongwana and Oliver Memani had joined forces and formed the United Crossroads Committee. Memani controlled one ward and Ngxobongwana had control of the other three wards of Crossroads.

The Koornhof Agreement had effectively handed both a free ticket to print money, as desperate people were required to pay them for the privilege of official enumeration and inclusion as original settlers. The lists grew longer and longer and with the limitation of space in New Crossroads, disputes arose between the leaders.

The influx continued and as allotments for settlement became sparse, satellite settlements sprang up and those allotments became subdivided, resulting by 1985, in the most densely populated single story settlement in South Africa. Crossroads was to become more densely populated in the coming years than anywhere else in the world, including the shantytowns of Mexico City.

Koornhof's New Crossroads development was planned to take place in three phases. Phase 1 was built in 1981 and comprised 1,100 housing units. Settlement beyond this was too fast and too lucrative for the leaders and there was no consensus as to who really qualified on those lists. Apparently, following another helicopter flight, this time shared by P.W. himself and Piet Koornhof, there followed a policy decision that all blacks would "voluntarily" move to a newly identified (by the famously pointed index finger of the right hand of the State President), settlement called Khayelitsha. And so, development in Crossroads was frozen and the planned phases 2 and 3, now known as KTC, became Memani's settlement area after he was eventually evicted from Crossroads phase 1 by Ngxobongwana.

At this time, shacks all over Crossroads were being demolished by the authorities with great regularity, often during cold, wet, winter months and also by the leader's henchmen when the disputation escalated. Many attempts at forced removal (as opposed to the idealised voluntary move) resulted in trauma and tragedy and so much pain for many families trying to eke out what could barely be described as an existence.

To make the move more attractive, squatters in Crossroads were offered a serviced site in Khayelitsha and an eighteen month temporary permit to live in the Western Cape but the majority refused, demanding permanent rights and that the Koornhof Agreement be honoured. As fast as those who did make the move, moved, so their old sites were quickly occupied by more squatters, led by new leaders, Christopher Toise, Melford Gwayi and Siphika.

Having evicted Memani, Ngxobongwana had named Jeffrey Nongwe as chairman of the remaining headmen in Crossroads. In 1984, Ngxobongwana became Chairman of the Western Cape Civic Association in recognition of his leadership role in the struggle against apartheid and for his progressive political stance – this recognition, coming from the political left!

By 1986, the government, having failed in their attempt to "upgrade" Crossroads (and reduce density by approximately one third), had abandoned the Khayelitsha resettlement programme.

The leaders of the satellite camps and their followers were driven out and a big part of KTC was destroyed. Ngxobongwana, who'd gone into "voluntary exile" in the Transkei whilst this was going on, returned to Crossroads after this and reorganised his committees and their representation. (Note: he was actually in prison). Amid mounting violence, the ousted leaders, Toise, Gwiliza, Jerry Tutu, Ntamo, Yamile, Cabingca and Siphika formed a counter committee, named the Western

Cape Squatters Association. Their mission was to undermine the leadership of Crossroads and Khayelitsha.

The Western Cape United Squatters of South Africa (WECUSA) was formed shortly after the demise of this committee and comprised of Conrad Sandile, Nongwe, Tutu, Toise and Gwilise. Their mission was to promote development in black communities through negotiation with local and provincial authorities. The relationship with the more formal civic body, the South African National Civic Association (SANCO) was very strained.

Private developers were brought in to build approximately 800 new houses in Crossroads and these were offered to local residents for sale. Naturally, they could not afford them and so they were offered to outsiders with more money. Another 874 houses, in an area named Unathi, were built with state assistance (these under the leadership of Ngxobongwana in his new-found authority alliance) and offered to residents for a monthly rental of R55. Ngxobongwana was elected mayor of Crossroads and with Nongwe as his chair of 21 headmen, moved into 1988 with tensions building.

Nongwe rightfully accused his mentor of selling houses to outsiders and unfairly favouring allocations of rental houses. He and 14 headmen broke away from Ngxobongwana and open warfare was declared. The term 'warlord' became attributable to the leadership regime of the time.

Many died and were wounded and over several months, houses in Unathi were burned down. Ngxobongwana resigned as mayor and left Crossroads with his followers to settle in Driftsands, near Khayelitsha.

In 1990, Nongwe moved into the leadership role but over the next few years also lost support. In 1991 the Buntubakhe ANC branch led by

Depoutch Elese , a returned uMkhonto we Siswe (MK) * trained soldier, in the Unathi area took control. By 1992 the youth in Crossroads began rcjecting patriarchal leadership styles and turned more towards the democratised activism espoused by Elese, who formed an alliance with a SACP branch led by Amos Nyhakatyha with support from residents of Boys Town/Section 2 of Crossroads.

So, tensions building became a cauldron of old leadership belief systems (tribal headmen with allegiances from area origination – most prominently the Eastern Cape) and new leadership of intra – party political allegiances, forged in the anti-apartheid struggle. Warlords and activists…and then there were the women!

In the middle of all this, somewhere in the mid 1980s, Ngxobongwana had spent a term in Pollsmoor Prison, in the foothills of the Constantia mountains. Nelson Mandela spent eight years of his prison sentence here, and it was in Pollsmoor Prison that he got to know his warden, James Gregory, well enough to establish a lasting relationship of trust and mutual respect.

It is believed by many that during his imprisonment, Ngxobongwana was "turned" into a government supporter and upon his freedom, aligned himself with the Black Management Committee of local government. The 1986 war between the "witdoeke" (translates loosely as white cloths/clothed) and the anti-apartheid comrades is well documented. It is also believed that the police assisted Ngxobongwana to regain control of Crossroads and one can clearly imagine the methods used to drive out all of his opponents.

We already know that murder and arson were committed. So who was killing whom?

Here, rumours of a "Third Force," an evil killing machine, comprised of trained military youth soldiers backed by the government to cause disruption and unsettle the townships creating disruption in the lead up to the 1994 elections, became rife. Anyone living there at the time did not debate the rumour. It was as real as the blood in your next door neighbour's back yard…or on their hands.

Simultaneously, in 1991/2 there were the taxi wars. With the huge increase in the population and no public transportation from the burgeoning townships and no regulatory planning, all you needed was a Toyota Hi-Ace which was originally designed as a 16 seater, to transport as many as 22 passengers at a time. Then you'd need to establish your turf or the routes along which you and a consortium of your equally unregulated mates would operate, and you'd have to protect this. These consortiums were often politically aligned, so there were IFP (Inkatha Freedom Party – the party of the Zulu nation) and ANC routes. Bloodshed was no stranger, this was violent and it is also known that the police had been involved. 13 policemen were charged in 1998 with complicity in taxi violence which rages on today. Nongwe was strongly connected to the taxi wars at this stage.

Mandla Maduna, one of Nongwe's "Big Eight" – remember the formation of WECUSA - was convicted of the 1993 murders of three people at Depoutch Elese's house. Nongwe features again, co-opted by the Crossroads Council to act for them in a spree of intimidation and shack burning in an attempt to force people to move from Sections 2 and 3 to Lower Crossroads. Again, the police chose not to intervene. People fled to what is now known as Vietnam and the surrounding areas. People were abducted and taken for beatings and interrogation by members of Nongwe's committee before being interrogated by the Internal Stability Unit and the Criminal Investigations Department (both associated with the South African Police force).

Push back from brave residents refusing to be removed, resulted in burning of more homes and more intimidation in 1994. This was the year of the new democratic elections in South Africa. Newly released prisoners trained by the Azanian People's Liberation Army (APLA), the military wing of the Pan Africanist Congress (PAC) and notably one Malambo Gxokwe (released in January 1994) trained comrade youths to kill.

Depoutch Elese, (remember he had been a soldier in the military wing of the ANC), joined the South African Defence Force in January 1994 as part of the transitionary force. Astoundingly, Ngxobongwana, who had by August 1994 been forced to flee Driftsands, joined the apartheid government's National Party (NP) to represent the NP on the Provincial Legislative Council.

In October, John Willem, a Boys Town leader and South African National Civics Association (SANCO) member and ANC treasurer, was shot and killed and his shack burned down. Amos Nkhakatyha was murdered on the 30th of November. By the end of 1994 it was evident that a criminal element was alive and thriving within Section 2 and the Boys Town areas.

Nongwe's fickle head had allowed him to be seen to be driving the Reconstruction and Development Programme (RDP) forum in 1994 in order to increase his legitimacy but soon it became evident that RDP money wouldn't be lining the pockets of the sycophants and tensions grew between the political parties of the ANC and the PAC. Gwayi and Elese were part of these tensions.

Simon "Fatty " Mqulwana died as a result of severe burn wounds inflicted when his house was burned down on 11th January, 1995. He had been a state witness in a murder case in which Elese and two others stood accused. Nongwe's guards were APLA trained youth.

In the run-up to the local government elections of 1996, Elese was recalled from the army and won candidacy for the ANC. Nongwe stood as an independent and was ultimately dismissed as a member of the ANC as a result. Elese won the election and Melford Gwayi was elected to represent Boys Town/Section 2. Toise stood and lost in his ward of Browns Farm.

After the elections with the installation of the legitimate council and the relationship between SANCO and WECUSA improving somewhat, the local RDP achieved a measure of success in development activities and in so doing, brought a number of disparate groups together.

Nongwe and a Mrs Ngozi, a PAC member, were expelled from WECUSA in 1997 and it was they who formed the Crossroads Residents Association, (CRORA), allegedly supported by Ngxobongwana and Gxokwe. CRORA set itself up as an alternative development programme allegedly backed by the Integrated Service Land Project (ISLP) – originally set up by the old provincial administration. This was highly plausible, given Ngxobongwna's allegiances.

The Women's Power Group which rose to prominence in January 1998 appears to have grown up out of this CRORA grouping, linking them directly to Ngxobongwana, Gxokwe and Nongwe. Women from political parties including the PAC, NP, ANC and the United Democratic Movement were actively encouraged to join up with them.

And so it was, by the beginning of 1998, that the full spectrum of political parties, the provincial council members and council members of the metropolitan City of Cape Town, the local civic associations, both formal and informal, the police force, the taxi associations and everyone in competition with them was involved in multiple layers of conflict, wrought from self interest. It was clear that a criminal element had arrived in town as well and they were going to take full advantage of this cesspool. There was money to be had in the Reconstruction and Devclopment programme and everyone was eager to get their hands on it.

In the middle, still trying to fight for survival and battling to get to an honest day's work, not knowing whether their homes were safe nor indeed, whether they would make it home alive, were the citizens of Crossroads and its surrounding settlements.

The social engineering initiated and then left by the apartheid government was a horrific failure and would bring about the continuing legacy of crime, violence and the negation of every human right for generations to come.

The questions asked by so many in the post development reviews, were;

- To what extent was the apartheid state involved in the manipulation of violence within these communities, assisting conservative squatter leadership to perpetrate criminal violence?

- How was such large scale violence not managed through the legitimate structures of government, (police, military, local and regional government, and the criminal justice system)?

- Or in some twisted way, were the interests of the warlords, the perpetrators, the same as those of this criminal government? Mutual interests in causing mayhem so that maximum benefits could be gained (income and power for the warlords, and political support from terrified voters for the government)! We know that the government backed the "witdoeke" vigilante forces so called "third force" activities, which resulted in people being

> forced to flee their settlements and to resettle, only to regroup their own retaliatory forces and thence to rebalance the spiral of violence which has so effectively and radically prevented any socio-economic development from proceeding.

Traditional leadership or "old school' warlords supported by the government needed to stamp out insurrections from the newly vocal and very angry "comrades" youth group. Greed for power and money by the warlords, coupled with an unholy alliance with the government's need to oppose any anti-apartheid political group threatening to overthrow them, made the alliance a logical one.

At the end of the day, in the 1994 elections, the Western Cape was the only province in South Africa to remain in the hands of the National Party (apartheid) government, the last mainstay of a bygone era for the country. So, for some, the criminal strategies had been a success but for the overwhelming majority of the people it was an unmitigated disaster as the spiral of violence took on a whole new level of evil. Mutual self-interest had placed us all in a dreadful place. Inevitably, more would die, more would be displaced and the trauma inflicted would continue to impact the future.

CHAPTER 2

MEANWHILE…

Chapter 2

MEANWHILE...

In 1980, I was in my third year at university although only my second year of study. It's safe to say that having been released from the prison of boarding school, to which I had been subjected since the tender age of eleven, my newfound freedom of expression in an open university at the beginning of 1978 was truly a baptism of fire. Most importantly, it was my first exposure to the truth.

Pretoria High School for Girls (one could not say Pretoria Girls High), was then and still is, an iconic school if you're looking at the tuition of young ladies and the incredibly broad offer of extra curricula activities. But in my six years there, from 1972 to 1977, access to newspapers in the boarding school was limited to the Afrikaans press, "Die Burger" - or translated, "The Citizen" newspaper. Crazily, the government had the cheek to start a newspaper in the late 70s early 80s called "The Citizen" in Johannesburg, in competition with the so called leftist English news of the Rand Daily Mail, South Africa's only true voice in the press at that time. Later, when this proved unsuccessful, they shut down the Mail and locked up most of their journalists.

If one was dreadfully keen to get news from "outside" you'd have to have some measure of courage as these Afrikaans papers were only placed on the hall table outside the boarding school mistress' study. If you took the chance to grab a read you could very well end up in the eye of a very frustrated spinster, whose prerogative it was to punish liberally and ask for explanations later. It was not worth it, considering the lengthy periods of punishment I was already enduring, being "gated" (sometimes for entire terms) in the boarding school for escapades which today would be considered hardly remarkable for a growing child.

Not that there would have been much in the Pretoria News – nor the English press. Notwithstanding the fact that Pretoria was the seat of the Apartheid Parliament, all press was suppressed. The only news being taken out of the country was that being sneaked to the BBC by "radical journalists" who, under the emergency regulations, stood every chance of being banned or arrested.

And there was no television until 1974. This had no impact on us at boarding school and, I am sure, not on anyone at home either although I recall many hours of study in front of the test pattern by my younger brothers during my school holidays. In its first years, I remember the test pattern being followed by the nightly news at 6, hosted and narrated by B.J. Vorster, the State President at the time, who spoke mostly in Afrikaans but every now and then would break into heavy, gravelly and laboured English. He was at pains to explain to all of us white citizens why we were at war with Angola, why our brothers and sons were "up on the border" fighting terrorists armed with Russian guns and trained Cuban guerrilla fighters. Actually South Africa had invaded Angola and we were well into South West Africa, allegedly ours at the time, and we were up to all sorts of tricks of our own on these borders. I know this because I had four brothers, many friends and my husband, all of whom served under conscription when they left school.

What was certainly not in the news at all was the unrest in the townships, the 1976 Soweto uprisings of South Africa's black youth protesting their segregated education and their rights to be recognised as human beings in the country of their heritage.

At school I focussed on sport and my friends and spent a lot of time trying to get myself expelled for bad behaviour! Upon my escape after my matriculation in which, quite miraculously according to my mother, I had achieved a university entrance, I was determined to do something with it. Having not expected this to be the case, my parents had not applied to any university for my tertiary education. This was not a surprise to me as my mother had openly stated that she did not expect much from me in comparison to my quite extraordinary siblings (and there were five of them to worry about), so I had taken the precaution of applying to the University of Cape Town as my first choice. Well, to my and every other member of the family's great shock, not only was I accepted for the Arts degree I had chosen, but also into the Baxter Hall residence for women undergraduates.

It took a few months to digest during which time my father applied for late acceptance on my behalf to the University of the Witwatersrand, as he wanted to keep me under his watchful eye, not trusting my eager exploration of liberty at the time. Well, I was not going to agree to this and all ready to embark on my independence in Cape Town, ignored his telegram;

"Geraldine STOP Go to D F Malan Airport STOP Flight SAAxyz STOP Paid ticket at information desk STOP Have got you into WITS STOP"

Two days later my brother David arrived in his Morris Minor 1000 panel van and dragged my trunk and a strongly protesting me back to Johannesburg.

So, it could be said that I did not start the academic year with any degree of alacrity but I was extremely interested in what was going on around me. There were black students working alongside us whites in every lecture theatre. There were lecterns staging speakers set up on the Great

Hall Steps and library lawns in between (and during) lectures and the world exploded in a freedom of speech never before experienced by me in South Africa!

I revelled in listening to what seemed to me to be totally logical, even if impassioned, discourses on the wrongs of our world and it was not long before I was an eager participant in the many organised stakeouts and peaceful protest marches. Often, these would be led by our lecturers and professors so this was not just the protest of a wasteful student body.

One protest was a changing point for me. Early in 1979 we, the Arts students, had arranged a number of piles of rocks on the library lawns in commemoration of the June 6, 1976 Soweto riots during which there had been many young lives lost. On top of each pile of stones we had placed wooden crosses as if they were funeral pyres. The engineering students came out en masse at lunchtime and set the crosses on fire, barbequing their sausages on our stones.

It was devastating. My brother was a mining engineering student and he would have to give me a lift home that evening. I cannot remember whether he refused to give me a lift or whether I refused to get into his car but I suspect I chose to walk the 50 odd kilometres home. I would have been at some risk in the early winter evening darkness, walking along a highway and through suburbs bordering on Alexandra Township. Had it not been for a man with dirty photographs of nude women stuck all over his car dashboard and on the visors who stopped and offered me a lift for the last 20 kilometres or so, I think I might not have made it back. He suffered a black eye for his trouble though!

Needless to say, the dinner table was a central argument station from that point onward and it was with some relief that I was packed off to the university residence of Jubilee Hall. This was reminiscent in so many ways of the boarding school I had so recently escaped that I was not going to last too long here. I was technically in my second year, although having to repeat two of my core subjects due to my diligence in the canteen bridge games, and yet I was accorded none of the privileges of second year university students in residence. This meant that I had to live with the university curtains whereas others more "senior" than me could replace these with their own furnishings! I had tried several times to remove them (folding them neatly and placing them in my cupboard) only to return to my room to find my own curtains trampled on the floor and the ghastly yellow baby poo ones blindingly rehung!

I was left with no alternative other than to suspend them on the broom stick from my eleventh floor window and set them alight never to be rehung again. Unfortunately, I had not calculated the effect it would have on the local fire brigade, nor the hysteria which followed such a revolutionary act. I was quickly removed from the residence and managed to rent an apartment shared with another revolutionary in the predominantly student suburb of Braamfontein.

This was close to the attractions of the Devonshire Pub, affectionately known as "The Dev" and alongside the great fun of student life, the probable cause of my second marginally successful year. I was to move into two communal houses in Johannesburg's suburbs of Lyndhurst and Norwood and we had a whale of a time together with lifelong friendships forged in total trust and mutual support.

Thus it was that I was to spend a fourth year in a three year degree. My father had fairly withdrawn his financial support of my university career by this stage and so I had by some means managed to secure a Transvaal education bursary (having stated my goal to become a teacher) and was now on my own.

I had a great friend who joined me in my third year. He was in his second. Elliot was to ensure that I would pass my psychology exams from that point onwards. He would sit with me in lectures, share notes and coach me in preparation for exams. In return, he asked me to teach him how to swim. At the time we had a swimming pool in our Norwood commune, so this was no problem for me…until the owner of the property came to do an inspection during a swimming lesson. I was carted off to the local police station accused of trying to "drown the garden boy" apparently evidenced by the fact that I was holding Elliot's head in the water! The dilemma facing us was ironic. Either I accepted the charge of attempted murder or life for Elliot was going to be made extremely difficult, since he did not have a "pass" allowing him to be in Norwood!

It was a no brainer for me. Elliot's mother had two jobs cleaning offices at night and he was forced to study by the light of street lamps in Soweto. He needed to do well and get ahead as his family was making great sacrifices for him to study at a good university. Luckily for me, playing along with these charges had my friends in hysterics and I think that I was released with no charges. There would have been some embarrassment in proceeding with them. Elliot was to continue educating me on the ravages of apartheid as we would be refused entry into the whites only bottle stores and banks etc. and this would not be the first and last arrest. But then, in our world this was a badge of honour, and daily, I became more deeply infuriated by the indignities inflicted on our fellow human beings.

In my sociology class, students would be arrested by plain-clothes policemen, having been tipped off by police spies. These were students whose studies were being sponsored by the Bureau of State Security, (BOSS). These spies had even infiltrated our student leadership bodies such as the National Union of Students Association (NUSAS). I recall one infamous and bitterly denounced Craig Williamson! Some were held for the mandatory three month detention without trial, some disappeared with no trace other than the time they had spent in John Vorster Square, the preferred lock up facility for political prisoners. Excuses that they had "slipped on a piece of soap, or fell from the 10th floor window, or died from a hunger strike" were all unbelievable but frequently used by the authorities, managing media interest.

BOSS agents would follow us around at night, taking the registration numbers of all cars at parties we attended and our telephone lines were being tapped. It did not worry us at the time as it was such a usual and common event, notwithstanding that today it would be considered a major human rights transgression. But we laughed it off, often offering a list of all of our names to the agents sitting in their cars, just so that they were sure that we knew they were watching us, watching them, watching us, watching them…

In 1982 I participated in an honours psychology major group, studying Dream Therapy. We were mainly working with transsexuals in this study and assisting our tutorial leader in her doctorate study of this subject. We had a number of very sensitive students who were in no way dangerous at any level but who, through their association with some of the activists in town, were watched, arrested, detained without trial and eventually made to turn state's witness in treason trials of their fellow students. It was understandable, given the terror with which the authorities were viewed at the time. I was lucky enough to escape this trauma but saw at least two of my co-students completely traumatised and broken by their experiences here.

By 1983, twenty three years of age, having completed my degree and having spent some time windsurfing for the earliest pioneers of the sport in South Africa and having completed a debut role in personnel management, I was fortunate to be given an opportunity with Trident

Steel. This was one of the biggest steel merchants in the country and part of the Anglo-Vaal group of companies.

At the time, job reservation was in full swing. This meant that all supervisory positions were held for white people only. It precluded black people from aspiring to skilled and semi-skilled positions. It meant that some of Trident's longest serving and most knowledgeable employees had only managed to earn the right to drive the overhead cranes (seriously, today this would be considered a highly skilled position given the gravity of safety accident potential), picking up and processing upwards of 40 tonnes of steel at a time.

I had another problem too. When the personnel manager was offered an opportunity to move into an operations role, I was given his job. There were no other women in senior management roles and whilst the men found this quite difficult to stomach, I remember feeling the wrath of the women who saw me as a young leftist upstart who had not done my time to earn the right to supervise them.

Even the MD had great difficulty in understanding why he should give me the use of a company car when his personal assistant, who had been with him for years, did not have this privilege. I decided to help him by stating that as all his managers were men the only difference was that they had something I did not. I could, however, have one of these any time I chose, I simply did not have to carry it around with me all the time! He was apoplectic with rage at the time but he grew over the years to tell this as a story of his own growth. I got the car.

Things definitely did not improve when the first decision I made, to remove racial segregation of toilets, was challenged by everyone, particularly the women. They had been perfectly happy for the black cleaners to clean their toilets but to share them was not going to be so easily done. The men were able to cope because job reservation meant that the location of toilets was limited to the steel yards for black men and all white supervisors could simply use the office facilities.

The introduction of a management development programme to breach the divide for black workers was strenuously resisted by all white employees at the time but it was an enormously fulfilling time with its moments of pure joy and pride and others of utter despair and horror. I recall one incident when the ultra conservative right wing yard manager called me to an accident scene, where an employee had been crushed under a reversing truck. He demanded that I complete all the documentation for the investigation before the police removed the body and refused me any assistance from the ambulance services. He wanted to see how I coped. Not very well, until I had the support of this poor man's co-workers who began to work with me quietly singing and humming a native requiem for him. Whilst we were being shouted at by the yard manager, they stood beside me ignoring his threats and the strength they gave me will forever remain one of the strongest motivators for me in facing future challenges. This moment and others shared with my liaison officer, John, throughout my six years there, was a foundational stone for me.

John Skosane had been seconded to me by the Managing Director, Ernie Behr, who had the foresight to see the need for change in the workforce structures. The recommendations of the Wiehahn Commission of 1980 had been legislated and this meant that our workers were rapidly becoming organised into unions who, as collective voices, were soon to dominate political influence (as the political parties of the struggle, the ANC, PAC and SACP were all banned). John had been Ernie's driver when he had started the company up as a small scrap metal dealer. He had had an accident damaging his back and it was for this reason and the fact that he had a full history of the growth of the company that Ernie thought he'd be good as a support to me. He was absolutely right, as it was John who was to give me an understanding of where our workers lived and what their lives were really like in the nearby townships surrounding Germiston. He knew and he taught me to know, the names and family histories of every one of the more than 2000 workers in our company and it was the best first lesson in human resource management that I was ever to learn.

It was John who took me to visit employees when they were hospitalised for workplace injuries in Thokoza, Thembisa and Baragwanath hospitals and I realise now the risk he exposed himself to in being seen fraternising with a management representative.

But I really do think we were friends. He was the only person with whom I could have any conversation about what was really going on in the yard and equally, what the pressures really were like inside the building. Together we had an alliance which grew to one of mutual respect. When my first son, James, was born in 1986, it was John who announced his arrival over the loudspeaker systems in the factory and who told me that the workforce had cheered as if with one voice. To have birthed a son as my firstborn was apparently taken as confirmation of my right to respect. It was an honour I cherished and I will forever be grateful to John Skosana for having the courage to be my friend and mentor.

I had joined the Industrial Relations Institute of South Africa and subsequently, in the mid 1980s, the Institute for a Democratic Alternative for South Africa (IDASA) and was regularly exposed to the thinkers who were allowed to voice their opinions in the resistance movement. These were organisations promoting dialogue across racial divides, holding the government bodies to account for activities increasingly reported in the South African and international press.

It was a time of great empowerment across the nation. You could feel the growth of the anti-apartheid movement in one's bones. There was a rumble of discontent rolling along at an increased speed as we travelled though the 80s dealing with union strikes, negotiations for wages and other benefits and ever improving terms and conditions of employment. Everyone seemed to become braver and braver as each day passed and the government's suppression of activists was exposed everywhere. Freedom songs, actors and artists became political vocalists and the wave of resistance grew exponentially.

The wave crested and crushed all remaining barriers with the unbanning of the ANC in 1990, followed shortly by the inevitable and rightful release of Nelson Mandela and others to reclaim their leadership of South Africa, bringing us into a democratic society in 1994.

My tenure at Trident Steel had come to a close in mid 1989 when we moved to Cape Town to begin a new life. We had had our second son, Thomas, in mid 1988 two months before his due date, having lost his twin five months into my pregnancy. Thomas had been interned in the neo-natal unit of the Sandton Clinic because his lungs had not fully developed and he had no sucking reflex. The saline drip with which he and other babies had been intubated, had been contaminated, purportedly through sabotage at the factory (we were only to find this out a year later), rendering him a very sick little baby. Whilst he blessedly survived, the other thirteen affected babies did not and he has quite a reputation within the unit as a survivor! There used to be a metre square poster of him, entitled "Thomas Coy, Head Boy!" in the front entrance, used to encourage scared new parents of neonatal babies, the message being…if Thomas could survive this, your baby can too.

But at the end of exactly one year in intensive care we were told that he could not survive a highveld winter with all the pollution in the

Johannesburg air and so we moved to Cape Town, literally overnight, upon his discharge from hospital. We were equipped with a heart monitor and lung function alarm, kindly sponsored by Old Mutual, as we were in no financial position at that stage to cover this cost. We had sold our house and after all the medical bills had been settled, we were back to square one on life's board of financial security.

Life was still segregated, no matter the progress in metropolitan cities. On the overnight drive to Cape Town, following Thomas' discharge, I was following my husband and our eldest son James. They were in Dave's business ute (a pick up truck) towing a trailer with Dave's wine collection – he had his priorities - and the two family dogs.

I was carrying clothing and Thomas, in the arms of our wonderful gardener, Simon Mahlangu. Simon had been trained in CPR as a necessity in looking after this tiny little baby, who although a year old was only the size of a three month old baby. He held Thomas, attached to his monitors, for the entire 1300km trip from Johannesburg to Cape Town. Aside from losing contact with Dave and James after about five hours, just outside Bloemfontein, Simon and I needed rest, petrol and breakfast in Beaufort West. We stopped at a petrol station and entered the fast food restaurant for bacon and eggs. I can still feel the incredible discomfort for Simon who would have been painfully aware of the stares we were receiving, the suddenly silenced conversations, the cold receipt of our order, the quickest service to get us out of there.

Simon had come to work for my father at the age of 16. He was a Zulu son of warriors, with a proud achievement in education to year 10. He needed work to help his family and, like so many, had been forced to leave his rural home and seek work in the big smoke. My father had built a small house comprising kitchen, bathroom and bedsit room on our 5 acre smallholding in Linbro Park, which saved Simon from living in the closest township of Alexandra. As a young intelligent man, he learned quickly and became one of the best gardeners I have ever had the pleasure to work with.

Ten years later, with my parent's move to the farmlands surrounding Franschoek, Simon accepted a job working for my husband and I in our newly built home in Paulshof. He created a beautiful garden out of bare earth for us and then when it became too small to keep him occupied, held several casual gardening jobs for neighbours and friends as well. He was married with his own children by then and welcomed all the extra money he could make as he was in the process of building a farm at home.

Getting back into the car on that cold morning in Beaufort West, I had to apologise to Simon for the racist indignity, yet again, that he had been forced to undergo on my behalf. We had a great relationship built over many years and we had often discussed the progress of political change in the country and what that would mean for him. He was stoic and always dignified in his responses to the changes ever hopeful that his life would be different and more prosperous. So that trip in transition is memorable for me in that this was the last discussion I had with one I trusted as a close family member, regarding exactly what it meant to be black and what it meant to be white in a world in which neither of us felt we fitted comfortably.

Simon had gained employment with Dave's sister, Elaine, and would be happily welcomed into her community of workers in Johannesburg, while we moved on with our lives.

Cape Town was a great move. Neither Dave nor I had any work as our move had been quite sudden and our preoccupation with getting Thomas well had not allowed us to make this a planned transition. All we had was a vacant house belonging to my mother into which we gratefully moved on the 29th of May, 1989, the day after Thomas' first birthday. We waited two days for our furniture to arrive as the truck driver had visited relatives on the way down to Cape Town and clearly thought nothing about how we were to look after our children! We did, however, have some very good wine to keep us company.

In July I was so excited to be considered for a consultancy opportunity for a company called Gouws, Woods and Partners (GWP) as an associate consultant. Even though it meant no guarantee of income I was eager to prove my ability in industrial relations and managerial development, having built a passion for this at Trident. Against the odds, I was made a partner of this business within six months and am forever grateful to the partners with whom I was so privileged to work for the next decade.

It was within GWP that my memberships of IRISA and IDASA opened up opportunities in community and business alternative dispute resolution. I was trained by the Independent Mediation Services of South Africa (IMSSA) to become a mediator, conciliator and eventually an arbitrator in industrial disputes, serving on all of their business and community panels until 1999. I was also appointed as a Commissioner to the Commission for Conciliation, Mediation and Arbitration (CCMA), taking my oath of office in November 1997, under Justice Myburgh, Judge President of the Labour Courts at the time.

Through my consultancy work and my dispute resolution work, I was exposed to a huge cross section of industry in the private sector, government and para-statal organisations, non-government organisations (NGO's) working in the communities and with trade unions on their development programmes. I was to grow a passionate change management business and also a deep interest in team development which has stood me in good stead throughout my career.

I was also often called upon to work in the facilitation of community development projects, often when multiple parties were deadlocked with conflicting interests. It was a time of enormous fulfilment for me and I was enthusiastic and energetically motivated to always succeed, no matter the odds. As a result, there were times when I was held hostage by a group who felt that by using me as a bargaining chip, their interests could be better negotiated but I never felt that I was in any particular personal danger, as my role as facilitator and an officer of IMSSA was respected. It gave me a sense of invulnerability which is a precious and intoxicating tonic. It fed my passions and put me in exciting places. I loved my work and was so fully engaged in it, I would often work 20 hours a day.

I worked with incredibly interesting people, from trade union leaders to local government bureaucrats, from boardrooms in large corporates, to small business owners and each experience built me into a more competent and self assured consultant. I was comfortable with the advice, guidance and confidence with which I was able to settle disputes, even in the most complex environments and this was definitely the happiest period of my career.

CHAPTER 3

FREEDOM

Chapter 3

FREEDOM

"Our deepest fear is not that we are inadequate. Our deepest fear is that we are powerful beyond measure. It is our light, not our darkness that frightens us. We ask ourselves, who am I to be brilliant, gorgeous, talented, fabulous? Actually, who are you not to be?

You are a child of God. Your playing small does not serve the world. There is nothing enlightened about shrinking so that other people won't feel insecure around you. We are all meant to shine as children do. We were born to make manifest the glory of God that is within us; it's in everyone. And as we let our own light shine, we unconsciously give other people permission to do the same. As we are liberated from our fear, our presence automatically liberates others."

NELSON MANDELA

There's a great book called "The Miracle of a Freed Nation" which reflects the metamorphosis of South Africa, visually, through the pictures taken by the Sunday Times news reporters, South Africa's largest newspaper of the time. It begins with then President F.W. De Klerk's opening of parliament speech on Friday, 2nd February, 1990, when he announced the "unbanning" of the African National Congress (ANC), the Pan-Africanist Congress (PAC) and the South African

Communist Party (SACP). He also announced that Nelson Mandela was to be released.

The rolling rumble of the 1980s had grown to a roar as the decade closed and international pressure, spelling out inevitable economic doom for South Africa if it continued on the apartheid trajectory, had finally forced a clumsy surrender. Whilst De Klerk's government had come to the conclusion that there was no alternative other than to submit to internal and external pressure for complete and radical change, there was an understanding that the issue now was to ensure a peaceful transition toward a future for all. The ANC and their alliance partners of the PAC, SACP and the Congress of South African Trade Unions, (COSATU) had agreed to a deal, brokered by politicians, academics and church leaders whereby all South Africans could face a future of equality and freedom without falling into a spiral of violence and retribution and counter retribution which was the greatest fear of the white electorate at the time.

It was the start of a new life for everyone. People who had been exiled from their country celebrated with pure joy as they planned their return, prisoners incarcerated with Nelson Mandela were jubilant in the expectation of their release and everyone inside South Africa, with the exception of the die hard conservative right, began to plan for a brighter future. It was a time of relief and also of some trepidation as no-one was naïve enough to believe that it would all go ahead without a hitch or two.

On the 11th of February, 1990, the very first picture in 27 years of Nelson Mandela was released. Previously, we had only seen his last picture, taken after his arrest in 1963 and then these had been silhouette drawings and shady caricatures drawn by people assuming aging factors just to give something to those of us desperate to have anything to reassure us that this mythical man was still there to be part of our future history. This first picture had our 71 year old Madiba standing tall in a blue suit, proud and lean next to F.W. at Tuynhuis, his official residence. The picture had been taken the night before, when the President had just informed him that he would be released the next day.

The gates of Victor Verster Prison in Paarl were thronged by hundreds and hundreds of people at 3 o'clock and camera crews from all over the world anxiously pressed the crowds for the best vantage points to record the turning of a new page in the psychological framework of South Africa. Flanked by members of his trusted friends and family (including Cyril Ramophosa) and holding his wife Winnie's hand, he walked out of prison to the cheers and love of all those who watched.

He was to be driven in an ANC cavalcade to the Grande Parade in Cape Town. Dave and I, anxious to see him and to hear his address, had travelled into the city from our home in St. James to participate in this extraordinary event. We were lucky enough to be squeezed into a side street and had the cavalcade pass by through the cheering crowd, touching his car as he went past with hope and joy. We finally ended up alternately climbing a lamppost to see him standing on the steps of the hall in front of the Parade.

Overwhelmingly, the feeling of all who were there was one of unity in a common hope, of joy in a fight well won. We were together as a nation joined in a single voice of support for the one man who could bring us together in a lasting way and which would give us back our pride.

As anticipated, it was not an easy ride; those fifty months in transition. Not for anyone. People had to learn how to unlearn their prejudices. These had been cemented in years and years of pain, horror, trauma, hype and propaganda. To do this, we had to go through a period of understanding how these sometimes unconscious beliefs made us say things and behave in ways where we were unconsciously prejudicial and hurtful.

I prided myself in my non-racist living but I had to discover things too. I remember one day describing to my friends how a "bloody drunk coloured man" had driven into the back of my car when I was on the coastal route between Muizenberg and Somerset West. I was asked if it would make a difference to my anger if this man was of any other racial group? "Of course it bloody well wouldn't!" was my reply and I remember my reddening face when I realised what I had said. It was deeply ingrained prejudice, with no relevance to me in my life, with no reason to be there, with a deep label of shame to be excised.

But this was trivial in comparison with the wars being fought in other places around the country. Few had anticipated the complexity of the deepest conflicts. Whilst the establishment of CODESA 1 in December 1991, the forum for the negotiation of a peaceful settlement had been characterised by the same inspirational wisdom and joy of the February 1990 freedoms, the negotiations themselves were a dismal failure. Madiba's marriage to Winnie Mandela was finished, due to a litany of well publicised actions which had made it impossible for him to keep holding on to her. The negotiating parties had reached an impasse on the percentage majority which would be required for a ruling party to effect constitutional change after the elections. Violence was breaking out all over the place with the ANC accusing the National Party of instigating it or, at best, failing to control it. The far left and the far right could not find middle ground easily and even cabinet ministers were falling over due to stress, (Finance Minister Barend Du Plessis suffered a nervous breakdown) and others (Gerrit Viljoen, although he was not personally implicated) cited fatigue as their reason for resignation when departments under their jurisdiction were charged with corruption.

People were still dying, left right and centre. Prison authorities were still torturing prisoners who were dying of their injuries and in the townships the so called Self Defence Units (SDUs), who were established to protect ANC supporters, were reportedly out of control. Negotiations came to a grinding halt in mid 1992 and the inevitability of the descent into the violent spiral became ominously real again.

With despondency settling in, everyone's eyes, hearts and ears were on the conduct of both F.W. and Mandela. Their relationship was showing strain but they had kept the dignity in their relationship even if it was clear that there was no agreement on many issues. It was only when Joe Slovo proposed a "sunset clause" offering the government a 5 year joint ruling role that the negotiations eased back into flow, even if it meant that not everyone was happy. It was the panacea needed to break the deadlock and recommit the parties to the table.

Trouble between the ANC and the Zulu nation's Inkatha Freedom Party continued unabated and although Chief Mangosuthu Buthelezi is no longer the maligned and ousted leader, it is still a prevalent source of angst today.

The National Party's Roelf Meyer and the ANC's Cyril Ramophosa were the chief negotiators and both distinguished themselves with growing respect across the nation as negotiations ensued but it did not stop the violence. Just as the centre parties strengthened their resolve to find a resolution and their relationships as a result, so the fringes on the right and left became more frenzied in their resistance. In April 1993, Oliver Tambo, the former President of the ANC who had spent so much of his life in exile whilst Mandela was in prison, died. Andries Treurnicht, the Conservative (right) Party leader also died. And on the 11th of April, Chris Hani was assassinated.

Chris, despite his chequered past as a controversial leader in the armed forces of the ANC's uMkhonto we Sizwe (Spear of the Nation), had grown his reputation as a much more moderate leader of the ANC youth and was a critical player in bringing this significant electorate along for the ride to the elections. His death sent shockwaves throughout the nation. Together with the loss of the respected and honoured Tambo, the killing of Chris Hani by the far right wing, left the gates wide open for the negotiating ANC to lead a walkout from the elections. This was a future too terrible to think about. Now ominously supported by Winnie Mandela, Peter Mokaba, a youth leader, was mounting a strong "kill the boer" campaign (translated as "kill the farmer" but really meaning everyone who could possibly be blamed for apartheid).

A march was organised along the N2 Highway and into the city of Cape Town, back past the very same Grand Parade, for ANC supporters mourning the loss of Chris Hani and it was to be a peaceful demonstration of defiance against what had happened. Again, thousands participated. It is a significant event since it was marked by calls for peace by Nelson Mandela, F.W. De Klerk and Archbishop Desmond Tutu, all of whom prevailed upon the people not to let the crisis derail the negotiation process but there were partisan groups who would see this as an opportunity to use this for precisely that reason. So whilst the mourners followed the rule, these outliers caused havoc, burning cars, trashing shop fronts in the city and generally trying to disrupt the peaceful march.

For the far right, it was a test of strength to see whether F.W. would order the police to intervene and control the attempted mayhem. Significantly, he failed the test because had he brought the strong arm of the (loathed) law down upon the legitimate mourners there would have been every reason for the ANC (being forced to publicly recognise the untrustworthiness of the government) to walk out of the negotiations.

For his failure he ran the risk of alienating the right (and potentially many of the white electorate who now feared an uprising of retribution) and it was a demonstration of courage to hold back and not (ab)use his so called legitimate authority of the police force. For this failure, he won the respect of the ANC and their partners in support of continued leadership towards the negotiated transition. It was a potentially massive stumble along our path toward freedom but it was a great example of leadership in negotiating strategy. Likewise, when working with teams in negotiation training, I and my partners would always use this example and that of Cyril Ramophosa's leadership in holding people to account in Codesa 2 and 3, as part of our training.

Again, incredibly, we had avoided a slaughter. South Africa's miracles were still happening.

Election fever gripped us all in 1994. Archbishop Desmond Tutu had coined the term, the "Rainbow Nation" a wonderfully warm, light and happy picture of South African people of all colours getting on with their lives in harmony. April 27th was the big day.

Still, there were hiccups. Buthelezi was refusing to play ball and was not coming to the party, refusing to participate and raising fears of violence in KwaZulu-Natal. Barely six weeks before the elections, violence had broken out in Mafikeng, the capital of the Bophutatswana homeland, with the massacre of three Afrikaner Weerstand's Beweeging (AWB – far right conservative) members who had invaded the homeland ostensibly in support of the leader, Lucas Mangope who was resisting the changes which meant that his homeland would be reincorporated back into South Africa. His unholy alliance with the AWB would normally have been viewed as comic relief but the dreadful massacre by a member of Mangope's police force on national television demonstrated yet another of South Africa's great ironies in social constructs. It also proved the futility of resisting change because after this we moved straight into the elections.

I had been appointed as the Mediation Co-ordinator for the Western Cape, which meant that I had to sit inside the allotted electoral commission offices and facilitate the communications from electoral centres around the Western Cape. My job was to arrange for mediators to settle disputes at these electoral centres where they arose between party observers on election conduct, protocols, distribution and collection issues and anything that made them unhappy. There were many in the offices with logistical planning roles and it was a busy time. Filled with pride and a sense of great purpose, we had covered our cars with Independent Electoral Commission (IEC) decals and these were considered passes to any of the communities, often inside the townships, where we worked. So whilst politicians kissed babies and made election promises few believed were keepers, there was generally an air of great excitement as the majority of South Africans prepared to cast their very first votes.

Much emphasis was placed on the transparency of the voting process because we simply could not afford any possible criticism, either internally or internationally, of our ability to run a free and fair election. Justice Johann Kriegler, a judge of the Supreme Court, was the man tasked with ensuring that this would be the case. His bilateral negotiations had, two days before the elections, ensured that the IFP would indeed be included in the elections, the concession being reached "for the sake of the nation." No matter, yet another miracle which was gratefully received by all as, again, it potentially avoided inevitable bloodshed. It also meant that IFP stickers had to be added to the voting papers at the last minute.

On the 26th of April people with disabilities were invited to vote as we were expecting long queues and potential delays on the big day of the

27th of April. This was proclaimed a public holiday as everyone struggled to get their votes in on this momentous, historical day, a day when they claimed their citizenship of their country. The 28th was also a voting day, to catch all the latecomers or perhaps anyone disappointed on day one.

In our Regional Operations Centre of the IEC, we took calls from metropolitan and rural voting stations. I had to deploy mediators throughout the Western Cape and sometimes call for backup support at stations where voters feared that we would run out of voting papers. There were calls from voting officials who stated that walls and fences were being pushed over by the crowds in their haste to get to the booths and we had to get people on the ground to reassure everyone that we would not close the doors until the last vote was cast. Whilst we were initially concerned that there would be violent breakouts, few did happen, tensions eased and we became increasingly exultant as the votes poured in with the mood and pride of these elections. Our people on the ground, sometimes flown into places by helicopter, reported that "peace be with you" was the more common refrain, as people greeted each other (black, white, coloured and Indian) as equals for the first time. We extended the voting days to include the 29th of April as our supply and demand logistics were sometimes hampered but overwhelmingly, the people were calm, settled, peaceful and tolerant.

Despite the fears that if we voted the ANC in with a 66% majority we'd wake up in a bankrupt country with our houses and property stolen from us and "redistributed" to those in greater need and lucky to escape with our lives, the gods were aligned yet again. The ANC and its incorporated COSATU and SACP alliances came in just short of it at 62.65%. The National Party came in at 20.39% and the IFP at 10.54%.

The ANC duly formed the "Government of National Unity" as agreed in the accord originally proposed by Joe Slovo and we South Africans were just happy to celebrate our newfound respectability in the world.

> "During my lifetime I have dedicated myself to this struggle of the African people. I have fought against white domination and I have fought against black domination. I have cherished the ideal of a democratic and free society in which all persons live together in harmony and with equal opportunities. It is an ideal which I hope to live for and to achieve. But if needs be, it is an ideal for which I am prepared to die."
>
> *NELSON MANDELA*
> *spoken from the dock in his Rivonia Trial of 1963.*

On Tuesday 10th May, another public holiday, kings, queens, emperors and heads of state took their places in the podiums leading up to the main stage in front of the Houses of Parliament in Pretoria, as Nelson Mandela was inaugurated as the State President. I can still feel the goose bumps as the transformation became official and tears of joy, relief, pride and honour as the South African Air Force Silver Falcons flew past spectacularly dropping their wings in salute as the crowd roared and roared again and again for our new leader. He had gone from treason prisoner to State President in his lifetime.

Those Silver Falcons are indelibly marked in my memory in the colours of their final vertical rise, behind and above the spectacular setting, as one of those pilots was my beloved youngest brother, Major Stephen Heugh. As the 55th team member (since its inauguration) and the youngest SAAF pilot to make the team as their breakaway pilot, he was flying his No. 5 plane. He was to demonstrate his amazing skills in 72 shows around the country before he left the Air Force to join South African Airways (SAA) as a commercial pilot. He would continue to do aerobatic flying which was his greatest love, "flying close to God" in his private capacity and giving lessons to those who sought to learn from his much respected skill. It was on one of these sorties on April 5th, 2005, that he died tragically in an accident over his beloved mountains above Somerset West.

They say that lightning does not strike twice but in my family, Stephen was the second of my younger brothers to die in a plane accident. Andrew, eighteen months my junior, had been killed when a freak wind took his glider into an inescapable plunge into a tree, as he brought it in to land on 16th February, 1992. Both of my brothers, very close to me, are wrapped in the wings of God, which is a reverence of pilots the world around.

"Oh! I have slipped the surly bonds of earth
And danced the skies on laughter-silvered wings;
Sunward I've climbed, and joined the tumbling mirth
Of sun-split clouds...and done a hundred things
You have not dreamed of...wheeled and soared and swung
High in the sunlit silence. Hov'ring there,
I've chased the shouting wind along, and flung
My eager craft through footless halls of air.

Up, up the long, delirious, burning blue
I've topped the windswept heights with easy grace
Where never lark, or eagle ever flew.
And, while with silent, lifting mind I've trod
The high untrespassed sanctity of space
Put out my hand, and touched the face of God."

JOHN GILLESPIE MaGEE Jr

Both of my wonderful and beloved brothers left behind their wives and between them, five children and our broken family; my mother, my two elder brothers and my elder sister. The pain does not go away and together with the loss of my father who died of a broken heart in 1995 (he had a brain tumour, but we believe it was the shock of burying his son that sparked the cancer's growth), following Andrew's death, there are gaping holes today in all of our lives. They say that time meddles with memories but I can remember with certain exactitude, those ghastly, painful ones that mark the soul. But I digress.

The bright colours of those plumes were those of a new national flag. Like the differences of our past, the old flag was packed off to history and we looked forward to this new rainbow nation.

The flag was designed to represent unity. The yellow, black and green were the colours of the ANC, (black for the people, green for the fertility of the land and the yellow symbolising the gold and minerals of the earth). The red, white and blue were taken from the colours of the Boer republics but anecdotally, have been said to represent the bloodshed of our country, the white people and the blue of the two oceans surrounding southern Africa. The last remnants of uncertainty in our futures were firmly negated by Nelson Mandela in the following months as he was quick to reassure everyone that private enterprises would not automatically become public ones and that property rights would be respected.

The election results in the provincial legislature were interesting in some ways and predictable in others. Predictably, KwaZulu-Natal remained the domain of the IFP and surprisingly in the Western Cape, 53% of the vote was won by the National Party, earning them 23 seats, with the ANC coming in second with only 33% of the vote and 14 seats. The remaining seven provinces, Eastern Cape, Free State, Gauteng,

Mpumalanga, North-West, Northern Cape and Northern Province were all landslide victories for the ANC.

Gouws, Woods and Partners, the business in which I shared a partnership with four others, concentrated on clients mainly located in the Western Cape. That's not to say that we did not work on contracts all over South Africa and on occasion with our clients in Zimbabwe and further north of our borders. These were heady days indeed as we were so well placed to advantage from every sector in the new South Africa. From state government to local government, the urgent need was for capacity building. Here was a newly elected leadership group of people who were very comfortable in community meetings of an informal nature and had been elected for their courage and leadership but had no idea of either provincial or local government.

Our partnership meetings, extending late into evenings in the remainder of 1994, were exciting and involved many of our associate consultants, all of whom brought strength and expertise to the table. We were building a Management Development Programme which we were to take right across the entirety of the Western Cape and then through the Northern Cape and finally through the Eastern Cape. Ultimately, this would tie me and one of the founding partners, Steve Woods, up for three years. It was an incredibly busy time for us as we had to maintain our private sector clients while continuing to build partnerships with other consulting teams, locally and internationally.

I was on top of the world at this point in my career. We travelled all over the three provinces, covering all of the beautiful and historical towns of the area we were working across. We drove thousands of kilometres as we worked through these three day courses, returning to towns to repeat courses for ever increasing numbers. We were exposed to all of the new leadership groups and many of the old guard; National Party and conservative right wing party officials who still clung to the wreckage of their political beliefs.

The challenge was to bring these local and provincial leaders together into a space where they could work collaboratively for the projects which their communities desperately needed in order to move forward. Often, we had to run these courses bilingually and as both Steve and I were English speaking our second language skills in Afrikaans left much to be desired. Luckily, this was often used as an opportunity to defuse the strain in the rooms as it put every one of us at an equal disadvantage in discomfort. There's a lot to be said for equal pain in the path toward gains! There was a lot of mutuality to be shared in the learning process and I remember these days with a great deal of warmth and affection.

The Reconstruction and Development Programme was a particularly prominent ticket on the new government's agenda and was well funded for its purpose of the redistribution of services and particularly utilities to communities so poorly cared for in the past. Jay Naidoo, previously General Secretary of COSATU, was the minister for the RDP portfolio and it would be to him that local government would have to appeal for support. It was for this reason that our capacity building programme was so necessary, as we often had to use real project plans as part of the course development to ensure that councils presented their best and most professional proposals. They needed to win against competing grant interests.

This work, together with my continued work as a mediator and conciliator for IMSSA, regularly brought me into contact with business leaders and union officials who had dual roles in local government. It was one of the amazing ironies of life in South Africa at that time and I am sure it is unique only because of the significance of the huge transition we were attempting to bolster. The leadership strength built within the union movement was a natural source for new political leadership opportunity.

For example, in late 1996 I recall strong strike mediations which I had to conduct up at the diamond and copper mines in the Northern Province, just outside of its capital of Springbok. On the diamond mine, I had had to be flown in a tiny six seater plane to the mine site, pass through their incredibly stringent security arrangements at their airport and was then supposed to travel in the mine vehicle to the meeting rooms. As a mediator, one of the most critical strengths to maintain was that of impartiality. To be seen to be driven into the mine in the Personnel Manager's vehicle would most certainly have compromised that view from the union's and worker's perspectives. I declined the ride, stating that I would walk the distance.

I had not considered that the airport was a good few kilometres from the office complex. I was carrying my briefcase with all my confidential briefing documents from all parties, part of the prescribed preparation for the processes and had thankfully sent my overnight bag with the management team. I was also eight months pregnant with our daughter, Rachel, at the time but I was committed to the purpose, so I set off.

Within a kilometre of my walk it became apparent that the striking workers had blockaded all the entrances to the mine office complex. I could see and hear the crowd in front of me and they were in full chant and toyi-toying to boot. This is a foot stomping dance accompanied by chanting of political slogans which had often been used in the political protests of our earlier anti-apartheid history and was often successful in intimidating the opposition. One can only imagine what these very seriously angry workers were thinking with the vision of a very obviously hugely pregnant woman, trotting along in the heat, clutching a heavy leather briefcase and moving it from hand to hand while approaching them with resolve. I don't remember feeling at all afraid. My work in the elections, all my work within communities and my industrial experience had me feeling confident in my ability to get out of most sticky situations. So I marched on, more thirsty and hot than afraid.

But I was not so well known in the Northern Cape at that time and these workers were angry. Mine security had always been successful at keeping everyone in line but now, due to the tensions and possible flare-ups, they were hanging back, unsure of what appropriate action to take. This would have been empowering for a toyi-toying crowd of angry male workers but there is something else which always amazes me in human nature. When such an absurd opportunity confronts us, we usually don't take advantage of it as we are forced to consider what the drivers and risks of the absurdity are. The result, in my case, was that the worker's simply continued to chant and dance as they encircled me and took me with them to the office block. This would have taken a good half hour as our progress was slow and the security details, completely at a loss as to what to do, followed slowly in their vehicles.

When we got to the conference room, together with the now frazzled management reps, I was met by the union official who was the regional COSATU representative and head of the National Union of Mineworkers for the Northern Province. He was also one of the councillors I had been training in Springbok on the MDP. When we recognised each other there was a hug and a kiss in greeting and lots of laughter and good humour from the workers. What fun! I had to work really hard to establish my credibility with the management team after that but we reached a great agreement resolving all differences over the next three days and nights of the mediation. Relationships were built on trust and that was definitely helped along by an easing of the stress and anxiety at the start.

It was often the case that leadership, baptised in the fires of apartheid, rose to the fore in the new South Africa. Where else would you look but to those who had been prominent in the years of the rumbling discontent? COSATU's leadership across all industries had been pivotal to the political expression of a people whose political allegiances had been forced underground. It was the union leaders who had stood bravely at the front of the firing lines of political voice. So it was no surprise that after 1994 the union movement suffered one of the biggest talent drains ever to be felt in the transition as their leadership was attracted into very big government roles.

Through my work, I had been lucky enough to meet and work with so many of the union heads and was to work with them again in their political roles. It felt like a privilege to do so and many of our training examples for negotiation skills came from these experiences. It was no surprise to anyone that Cyril Ramophosa, previously Secretary General of the National Union of Mine Workers of South Africa (NUMSA) became the lead ANC negotiator for change to the National Party's Roelf Meyer in CODESA 1, 2 and 3.

And it will be no surprise to me if we indeed see him take up a much more meaningful leadership role in the future of South Africa. We have already seen him grow into one of South Africa's most successful businessmen.

CHAPTER 4

1998

Chapter 4

1998

In retrospect, I think of this time as the top of my career. I was where I wanted to be, doing the work I wanted to do, trying to make a difference and a meaningful contribution to my world. Everybody dreams of this I know, to the point of it becoming a social cliché, but the work we were doing in the rebuilding of a nation was important.

There were International Labour Law Conferences often addressed by members of the ILO, there were National IMSSA conferences, National Peace Secretariat Conferences and Cape Town University Business School liaison meetings. It was an exciting world of constant learning and stimulation for me in addition to my work. Our clients were public and private sector organisations, Non-governmental organisations (NGO's) and not for profit community organisations and we were often at the front end of policy formulation on social issues. With one of the partners, I had worked strenuously to ensure that the advent of HIV in the workplace was managed in a caring and humane way, well before legislation had defined work practices in this area and I will always be proud of this work.

My family were happily growing and with my husband's strong support, we were apparently able to balance everything I was doing into a manageable stretch.

One of my clients in 1995, 1996 and through into 1997 was the City of Cape Town's Metropolitan Transport Planning Committee. This committee was comprised of a group of engineers, town planners, public and private transport officials, consulting engineers in transport and

Regional planning, as well as councillors with an interest in transport. I had been engaged as a facilitator for the committee which had multi party interests at stake and my job was to find common ground and ultimately agreement on future development. We had cast our eyes forwards in a bid to supplement the City's Olympic Bid for 2004. Different tiers in government, Provincial National and Local government bodies made the planning components strategically complex in policy development.

All of the committee members were men. There were strict and formal protocols for doing business. There were tea times, served by a tea trolley delivered to the boardroom at specific times and lunches served with the same precision and inflexibility. There were 24 to 28 members of the committee dependent upon the agenda being discussed. The chair and my client, was a brilliant engineer but a bureaucrat with little interest in the social niceties that must accompany such a gathering. It fell to me, the only woman in the room, to settle, intervene and get around inflexible time breaks when deep discussions on politically sensitive issues really needed to be given time to ease into agreement. Needless to say, the task was challenging but I remember really feeling that because I was different to them all I was given latitudes which advantaged my role.

I was becoming very different week by week. As we approached the end of 1996, my third pregnancy with our daughter, Rachel, was becoming more prominent, just as we were reaching the last stages of the draft plan. Rachel was born on the 9th January in 1997 and the next committee meeting was on the 12th. I had no choice. I wanted to finish the job and I was not going to let the client down. I can see their faces now as if it was yesterday. There was a general sense of shock as in I walked in with the baby in her portable car seat, together with all the other paraphernalia required by all new mothers. I must have looked like a packhorse and somewhere out of the mass of distributed items all over the floor next to my very formal seat at the boardroom table, I fished out my documents file.

Seated, I introduced a new member of the committee, who was duly entered onto the register of attendees by the committee secretariat. From that day onward, until the completion of the contract, Rachel was to receive copies of the minutes complete with references to when she expressed an opinion in loud and unmistakable volume, as well as when she recorded no comment to items challenged!

To do them credit, these gentlemen of state and city, grew to take it in turns to pass her around during committee meetings and some were known to argue for time with her. They even broke protocol to ensure that feeding her took precedence over tea and lunch breaks and so, in a funny kind of way, my daughter, the second female to be introduced into that particular boardroom, made a great difference from the time that she was just three days old!

> "I will not die an unlived life. I will not live in fear of failing or catching fire. I choose to inhabit my days, to allow my living to open me, to make me less afraid, more accessible; to loosen my heart until it becomes a wing, a torch, a promise. I choose to risk my significance, to live so that which came to me as a seed goes to the next as a blossom, and that which came to me as a blossom, goes on as fruit."
>
> *Dr DAWNA MARKOVA*
>
> An inspirational leadership development thinker

I was confident then. I was happily assured that I was making a difference and I believe I was respected for that. Our business was growing from strength to strength and whilst some of our partners were moving into very strong niche markets, Steve Woods and I had grown very close to another consulting company based in the UK, under the directorship of one Terry Murphy. He had been working co-jointly with us on a number of projects, his focus being on the development of teamwork and leadership at executive and mid-level management. There was a strong alignment with the work we had been doing in provincial and local government and we liked working with each other. We were, that year in 1997, to break up the Gouws Woods and Partners Group and start up The Achievement Network Africa, (TANA). We joined forces with another partner, Alfred Mahlangu, who we were hoping to entice from part time consulting (he was employed in senior management with Shell SA at the time), to a full time role, just as soon as the business we were touting for was contracted. This was a Change and Transformation agency and our relationship with Murphy's UK company gave us opportunities to work internationally with his other partnerships in Canada, Japan and Australia.

This was in its infancy stages as we entered 1998. We had our strategic planning meetings at our home offices either at Steve's home in Hout Bay, or at my home in St James, our hours dictated by our ongoing workday commitments and those of Terry's travelling.

I was still intrinsically involved in the MDP together with my commitments as a mediator through IMSSA, as well as a serving Commissioner to the Commission for Conciliation Mediation and Arbitration (CCMA). It fell largely to Steve, Terry, and Alfred to develop the business plan for TANA's future, so I was not yet practically harnessed by the clients they were building. I was working 20 hours a day at the time, very focussed, enjoying it immensely and very driven to deliver great outcomes. There were conflict management issues in almost every client framework, but I was as proud of my success in mediation, as I was of the development work we were doing.

The first call for the biggest change to my life came in late March 1998. Tensions were building in Crossroads, people were being killed. The City of Cape Town had approached IMSSA for a Community Conflict Mediator and the referral came through to me. I turned it down. I simply could not see myself taking this on in addition to the load I was already carrying. I did not feel that I could give it the attention it deserved. I was well aware of what it would take as I had been involved in some of the mediation work emanating from the Taxi War facilitations and I knew there were ongoing issues. They were deep, historical, and would require the complete and focussed attention of a skilled practitioner to manage them. They were big shoes to fill. In 1993 Justice Richard Goldstone had attempted to work through these tensions and to settle them. For all these reasons, I was convinced that I would not be the right person for the job.

Late April saw the second call come in from the IMSSA's executive head in the Western Cape. Again I refused, for all the reasons cited before, still firm in my belief that there would be others more capable than I to do the job and give it the attention it deserved. I learned that Andrew Boraine, the Cape Town City Manager, had requested me to do this work, having been referred from other work I had done for the city. I was beginning to feel uncomfortable, as my natural sense of duty was calling and I felt I was letting the side down a bit, but I had refused, so I was moving on.

Then around the middle of June, I received a call from Mary Simons who was very well connected politically through her own work and that of her parents, to some very important people in the New South Africa.

I had worked closely with Mary during the 1994 elections as we served together for the electoral commission. She told me that our President had asked her to personally seek to engage me for this project, as it was of such significant importance to the peaceful rebuilding process for the City of Cape Town.

Mandela was then in the throes of handing over his leadership of the ANC, (and working towards the 1999 elections where he would hand over to his successor) and ultimately, the Presidency.

It's important to recall too, that the Western Cape remained at that time governed at a provincial level by the National Party of old.

I knew it was important. I could not have refused. I, like millions of others in South Africa and globally, revered this man. If he wanted me to help matters along, who was I to refuse? I was reasonably confident that as long as I kept to the mandate requested of me, to design and facilitate the building of the peace structures as a consequence of the Commission findings, I'd be able to do a good job. So whilst I was reluctant, it was terrain I knew well.

On the 19th June 1998, the City Manager formally announced the Executive Committee of Cape Town's decision to appoint an independent and impartial commission of enquiry which would investigate incidents of conflict in the Crossroads and subsequently, Philippi areas. Council's service delivery programmes to these areas were being adversely effected by these conflicts and matters needed to be taken in hand.

Allegations had been made that the conflict over the previous five months within these two "suburbs" of Cape Town was driven by the conduct of councillors of the city of Cape Town and some of their employed officials, by community organisations and by individual members of the public. So who did that leave out, I wondered?

Essa Moosa, a lawyer who had served Mandela personally in preparing for his release in 1994, was to chair the Commission. Reverend Mlamli Mfenyana was to serve alongside me as the second and third Commissioners. He was a leader of the community, in his religious capacity at the time and much revered for his and his wife Freda's participation in the 1982 "Nyanga Squatters" protest fast. 57 men and women had taken refuge in the St Georges Cathedral of Cape Town, where they quietly and with dignity, fasted for 23 days in their fight for the right to live and work in the Crossroads, Nyanga and KTC areas including Modderdam and Unibel areas. The Reverend served alongside the Archbishop of Cape Town at the time, the renowned and much loved Desmond Tutu and his credentials in the fight for justice and equality for a sense of place and of belonging, for a home and a family in an unjust apartheid were impeccable. Our support team included Bulelwa Tinto, a senior member of the ANC Women's league and now member of the National Assembly and a charming and delightfully helpful fellow by the name of Jonguyiso Dyabasa. Their role was to provide us with administrative, logistical and secretarial support services with effect 1st July 1998.

I was in incredible company, and I knew that my appointment to this Commission was going to test me.

Our terms of reference - a direct transcript of that given to us upon our appointment were as follows;

"Your brief is to establish in a private enquiry and thereafter to submit a report on:

1. The nature of the allegations being made.
2. Whether there is any substance to those allegations.
3. What appears to be the primary and secondary causes of the conflict.
4. The persons and/or groups and/or economic and/or social factors responsible for the causes of the conflict.
5. The extent to which the conflict is impacting on the City of Cape town's service delivery programme; and based upon your findings;
6. To recommend mechanisms that could be instituted by the City of Cape Town to
   - minimise future conflict;
   - alert the City of Cape Town to possible future conflict situations;
   - channel future conflict into a constructive mediation process; and
7. To indicate what the prospects are of succeeding against;
   - Officials of the City of Cape Town in terms of a disciplinary hearing under the Labour Relations Act;
   - Councillors of the City of Cape Town in terms of the Code of Conduct under the Local Government Transition Act;
   - Community organisations and individual members of the public in criminal proceedings if your findings are made available to the South African Police Services.
8. The final report should also set out;
   - Terms of reference;
   - Scope of Enquiry;
   - Evidence;
   - Analysis of Evidence;
   - Findings and Conclusions;
   - Recommendations."

Notwithstanding all my initial reticence when I read these now, I cannot believe the breadth of these Terms of Reference and could kick myself for my naiveté and lack of attention to the detail this would require in order to deliver to them.

Naturally, I had gravitated to the points six and seven above, these being my core skills areas. I was confident about the recommendations for the management of conflict, past, present and for future management. I knew my way around the Labour legislation and certainly, I had had a lot to do with the Local Government Transition Act. I was assuming that my fellow commissioners would be more than able to deal with the former points. Essa Moosa would be most familiar with the processing of evidence and dealing with the evidence toward the findings, and from the Reverend's intimate knowledge of the players in the community, I felt we were well placed as a Commission to fulfil the task at hand.

Between the date of the announcement to Council of our appointment, and the beginning of the hearings, the communications plan went into frenzied activity, as there was no time to be lost. 200 posters, 150 in Xhosa and 50 in English were placed at Police Stations, schools, libraries, clinics, shopping centres and on poles in both the Crossroads and Philippi areas. Pamphlets were delivered to every household, door to door. Media began printing reports of the Commission engagement and hearings process. There were three television broadcasts on the SABC's "Cape at Six" programme and Radio Xhosa and Radio KFM provided coverage of the process throughout.

We knew that we had to be as transparent about the process as possible in order to ensure that people would trust us to speak openly and we were also well aware that there would have to be different ways for us to access these people, or vice versa, given that they may have to take significant risks to talk to us. So we offered three different means –

written submissions, (which we received throughout the four months of the enquiry), statements transcribed by our secretariat and the enquiry hearings themselves.

We began these hearings on 16th July 1998….

CHAPTER 5

STRANGE BEDFELLOWS

Chapter 5

STRANGE BEDFELLOWS

From the police reports supplied to the commission, the statistics were stark. From the beginning of the conflict in January, to the date of the report, 5th November, 1998:

Crossroads cases	Browns Farm (Old Crossroads) cases
11 murder (13 killed)	6 murder (9 killed)
45 arson	8 arson
21 attempted murder	18 attempted murder
3 malicious damage to property	1 malicious damage to property
3 intimidation	
5 housebreaking and theft	2 housebreaking and theft
2 theft	1 theft
	4 possession of unlicensed firearm
	2 common assault
	1 pointing a firearm
Total Case report = 90	**Total case report = 43**
Cases on Court role = 54	**Cases on Court role = 37**
No convictions at the initiation of the enquiry	

Cape Town City Council wanted to build the houses promised to the people in the Reconstruction and Development Programme, supported by the Provincial Government and definitely in the interests of service delivery for the Cape Town Metropolitan Council. The conflict, distilled down to the bare rubs, could loosely be described as pro-development vs anti-development. Beneath the apparent disagreement on the progress of housing development in the area, political aspirations and old rivalries drove patterns of violence which would only escalate in coming months. The full spectrum of all represented political parties seemed to be involved.

Crossroads was bounded to the north east by the Cape Town International Airport, to the south east by Philippi and the west by Nyanga. Depending on who you talked to, Crossroads was often referred to as Old Crossroads or Lower Crossroads. The N2 Highway formed its northern boundary and Lansdowne Road, its southern boundary.

For development purposes, Crossroads had been numbered in phases 1 to 4. I have already described it as the most densely populated (per square metre) in the world. With no sanitation services, council was still forced to collect waste from buckets behind informal houses/shacks at night, known as night soil collections. Vehicular access was almost impossible given the proximity of all the dwellings to each other.

Formal housing, as we know, had already been built in Section 1 (Unathi) and also in part in Section 2 (Boys Town), with 42 square metre houses. Attempts were now being made to build houses in phase 4.

The torch was taken to the tinder in January 1998. The Crossroads Women's Power Group occupied the Crossroads administrative offices, unseating the officials, ostensibly in protest against the size of the houses being built. More on this later.

Several attempts had been made to evict the women. All had failed. The courts believed that the situation should be settled by the Cape Town City Council. The police station, who council reverted to once their own officials had failed through normal administrative channels, was awaiting the appointment of a new station commissioner and the police were reluctant to get involved in the rising tension because their actions in the past had been seen to be biased (correctly) and were without a leader to instruct them. So, no action had been taken. Five months into the year, at least ten people had died and some forty people had lost their homes to arson. By the time the new commissioner, Director Mpembe, was appointed the situation in Crossroads had reached boiling point. Although more decisive action was being taken, there was a lot of confusion as to the legitimacy of that action given the involvement of members of council, the Reconstruction and Development (RDP) local committee and leadership within political parties.

For example, on 29th March, Jeffrey Nongwe's son, Xolisile, was stabbed to death in Gugulethu in what was described as a gang related incident. In April alone, the RDP Chair, Stulo, had been slain together with Kupiso, both ANC and RDP executive committee members. Stulo had been a member of the "Big Eight" gang and in 1993 had been on Nongwe's bodyguard/hit squad. But after the local government elections he had withdrawn from both Nongwe and his newly formed CRORA and as a committed ANC leader he had shown leadership within the RDP local committee and brought relations between WECUSA and SANCO back onto a more even footing. Killing him was a loss for the development initiatives in Crossroads.

Then on 9th May, Thembelani Ngozi, son of Sylvia Ngozi (PAC and founding member of the WPG) was shot dead. He was allegedly the leader of the APLA/"Qibla" youth hit squad. Houses were burned down in retaliation for this over the next few days and at his funeral on 30th May his grandmother was shot in counter-retaliation and two other funeral goers were seriously injured. At the same time councillor Gwayi and his son had been arrested in connection with arson and community leaders had been chased by armed youth out of the areas of their leadership. Councillor Elese reported to the police that the funeral had been patrolled by Qibla youth provocatively waving their firearms around. Two attempts to kill councillor Elese had been made in May, so it was no surprise that not much love was lost between him and anyone related to the Women's Power Group and their related affiliates.

A march for the Masakhane Campaign (this was an ANC initiative led by a cross section of social and sectoral groups, including religious leaders, initiated in 1996 to encourage communities to pay for services received; water, electricity etc.) had to be aborted as reports that armed youth linked to APLA/"Qibla" were guarding the Women's Power Group at the administrative offices. Had there been a confrontation between the WPG and those marching for the Masakhane message, there could have been bloodshed.

On 9th June the Cape Times and Argus newspapers printed articles announcing the launch of an urgent investigation into all of these events.

Meanwhile, in a more sedate Cape Town…

Ironically, as part of the Transport Plan in which I had been involved, I had led a group of the city engineering team into the townships adjoining the airport to engage the community in the planned extension of the runway system which would impact some of the homes in the flight path. Unbeknownst to us, the city had decided to turn off the electricity to some of the areas that day as services were not being paid for and so we were faced with some very angry residents. I think there were five of us in total, two interpreters, two engineers and myself.

Not only did we not get to deal with our presentation but we were very quickly relieved of all our equipment - flipcharts, overhead projector, screen and all our stationery and computers and phones. These were the least of our worries. Our exit was very definitely blocked and it becamc apparent that we were to become the bargaining chips to get the electricity resupplied.

Facing us in the hall were all the men. The women were not inside the hall but seated outside in a gathering force, in the entrance to the town hall. Whilst we were receiving a lot of strong feedback inside the hall, my advice to my clients was to hold back, stay calm and not to show any fear but rather reassurance that whilst we were not part of the electricity decision/department we would do our very best to prevail upon council to do the right thing. I was observing the communication between the men and the women and it became very clear to me that the instructions were coming from the women. They were very definitely calming the men and insisting that we were not to come to harm. At that stage, I had no understanding of the Women's Power Group as I had not yet been engaged by the commission but I am glad that I had had this insight into their activities at the inception of my appointment.

As it turned out, I appealed directly to the women that night and it was they who prevailed upon the men to release us in the early hours of the morning, returning only our car keys to us, on the understanding that we would indeed get the City Council to review the issues surrounding service delivery. Little did I know that this would prove to be the lesser of the key drivers in what was to become a much more violent protest.

By July, 82 cases of violence had been recorded by the police.

It's useful to revisit some of the continuing patterns in history. The conflict, which began in 1986, founded on battles for territory and power, continued. Those who held the power to control through government concessions, held the power for the allocation of sites and the financial returns for the same.

Those who assumed leadership positions within informal settlement areas in the new South Africa looking to development, often found themselves in conflict with those who would have much to lose in the development of structured housing where rates and taxes would have to be paid for service delivery and no longer to the traditional leadership. Sometimes, these were the same people!

Councillors Gwayi and Elese, both of whom had traditional power as well as new civic power, were both directly involved in the violence. Together with the executive committee of the RDP forum and members of the Provincial Administration they sat on the Project Committee for Development in Crossroads and were responsible for site allocation for Phase 4 houses to be built - for and on behalf of people from Section 2 and 4 of Crossroads.

You will also recall the infamous Ngxobongwana; well, he was now a member of the provincial parliament and there was an expectation that he would be bringing in votes in the 1999 election for the National Party. If he did not, he'd be ousted from this cushy leadership job. It was believed at the time that due to the political unlikelihood of him getting many National Party votes he was looking for a new home, possibly within the United Democratic Front and as he had a traditionalist following, it was easy for him to make promises to members of the Women's Power Group which would gain him those scarce votes.

Both Ngxobongwana and Jeffrey Nongwe perceived the loss of power (and income) and had apparently joined together in yet another unholy alliance with strong armed support. Both had a relationship with

Christopher Mtshutsmsi Toise. He was the traditional leader of the Philippi East and Old Crossroads settlements, also originally from the Eastern Cape, also a warlord but having come up against the law and the "witdoeke" of Ngxobongwana's armed vigilante groups in the earlier years, had been ousted from Philippi by his previous compatriots.

So there was a mish-mash of allegations and counter allegations being made by groupings of people who were so politically disparate, of interests at odds with rational thought, of no law and order, no investigations and no charges being laid, of partisanship and fear. It was heart breaking to see the suffering on the ground by people who just wanted to get ahead with a future they had fought so hard for but which was being denied them by the greedy, by the criminal and by their own new leaders.

The police admitted to the allegations made that they had taken no definitive stance. They were afraid to do so as their credibility had been brought into serious question and they were under considerable constraint with regard to resources, both in terms of personnel as well as vehicles. This was understandable, given the Western Cape Regional Services Council guesstimates of between 50 and 60 000 people in the Crossroads community in 1990.

It's also a good time to remind you that SANCO, the South African National Civic Association and WECUSA, the Western Cape United Squatters Association, were the opposing parties wrangling over the RDP funds which were supposed to be used to develop the communities. SANCO was the officially recognised body. WECUSA had fronted as the alternative development forum and later, when Nongwe was kicked out, he led his followers into the Crossroads Resident's Association. CRORA was in opposition to the RDP's attempts to promote development even though some of its members were ANC alliance members too. It was this defiance that built strange bedfellows.

For example, Jeffrey Nongwe, although he claimed to be a member of the ANC, as a leader of WECUSA and then the morphed CRORA had all the while remained aligned with the National Party through the Cape Provincial Administration – the authority which administered local government. A bit like having a foot in a couple of canoes!

He was also something of a church minister on Sunday mornings and was regularly identified as the leader of groups accused of intimidating people in Section Four (Unathi), the developed area of Crossroads, as well as extortion. He'd collect R20 (twenty rands) from each household to set up a branch of CONTRALESA (Congress of Traditional Leaders of South Africa) and then retain the money for his own use.

Like Ngxobongwana, he was concurrently a paternal leader known for his ability to talk and lead with personality and a bully and killer with no conscience. There seemed to be no end to the wickedness that these blokes could get up to and there seemed to be no-one who would man up to manage them. By mid 1998, there was a sinister energy prevailing over the whole of Crossroads and Philippi East, Browns farm.

CHAPTER 6

THE WOMEN

CROSSROADS CRISIS

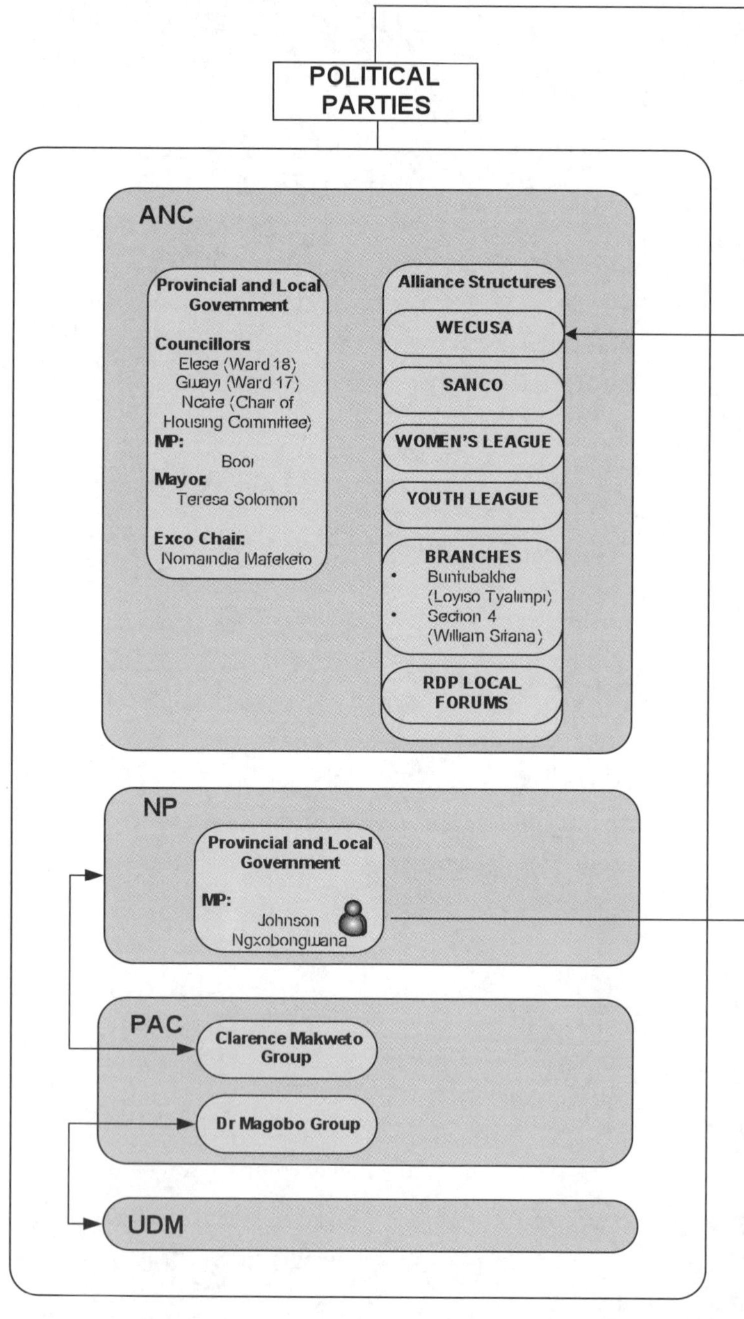

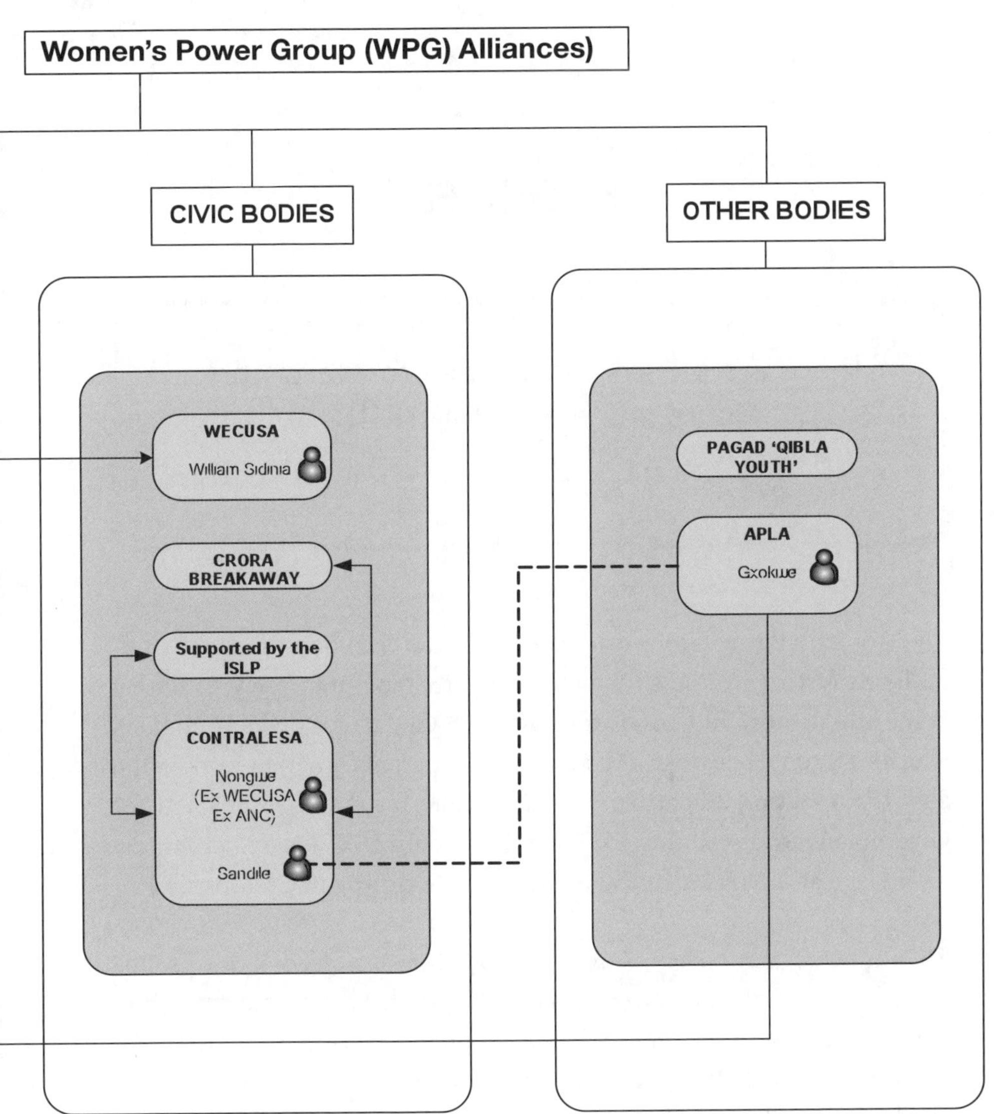

Party/Group to Party/Group Alliance	◄──────►
Person to Person Alliance	- - - - - -

Chapter 6

THE WOMEN

"There are always three sides to every story... yours, mine and the TRUTH."

UNKNOWN

The Women's Power Group originated from the "Mothers of Crossroads" in the early years of the struggles for tenure, the right to stay, to have a home and to work in Crossroads. By 1995 they had trained as mothers who could run day care centres/crèches for parents going to work in the city. It's no surprise that the "sit-in " venue for the 1998 demand for government accountability for funds for undelivered housing promises, took place at the IKAPA local administrative offices in Crossroads.

So who were they? They were a group of multi party interest groups from different political parties, which had been birthed through the civic bodies, supposedly in support of development housing in Crossroads. Because they had allegiances to old traditionalist leadership, they were "looked after" through the PAC and NP political alliances, by the armed "Qibla" youth – related to PAGAD (People Against Gangsterism and Drugs) and also the youth wing of the old APLA army. Whilst this is confusing enough as it is, there was another strange element which had crept into the picture.

PAGAD had started out in Cape Town in 1996 in the Cape Flats as a handful of neighbourhood watch type vigilantes. They wanted to put pressure on the government to more effectively address violence, gangsters and the illegal drugs trade. At first, they had been received quite well as there was a lot of empathy for anyone who wanted to make a point that the police force was not doing a good enough job but by 1998 their modus operandi of setting fire to gangster's houses in order to kill gangsters and drive by assassinations, took on a whole new life of its own.

Instead of being regarded as a partner in fighting crime, this group now attracted gangsters, using this premise to protect their territories and their own illegal dealings, so it became a war of gangsters. They were also charged with the bombings of synagogues and gay nightclubs and famously, on the 25th of August, 1998, of the bombing of Cape Town's Planet Hollywood. By this time they were regarded rightfully as a terrorist group and were feared by the local citizenry.

Their interest in Crossroads? Where there was development money to be had, for the building of houses and developers who needed protection, who else was better equipped than a group of armed vigilantes who could extort a price? Hell, why bother with protection rackets when you could infiltrate the development company yourself and thus gain direct access to the funds? Big statements, but truly considered factual as we progressed through these commission hearings.

So, back to the women. They had occupied the Crossroads administrative offices in January. They were said to be a group of about 300 members although there would only be as many as 30 involved in the sit-in at any one point in time.

Mrs Ngozi, who had been expelled from WECUSA in the latter part of 1997, together with Jeffrey Nongwe had allegedly started CRORA, which we know was supported by the traditionalist warlords Ngxobongwana and Gxokwe, setting itself up as an alternate development programme, allegedly supported by the Integrated Serviced Land Project (ISLP) – and this group had been set up by the old Cape Provincial Administration. The Women's Power group grew out of this, with links to all the political parties, PAC, ANC, NP and UDM.

It was this group who, before the commission, argued that the houses being built were not big enough and they whose members refused to move from their shacks so that no houses could be built. It was this group whose criminal supporters sabotaged machinery and prevented the developing contractors from building. It was this group that accused the two councillors (Gwayi and Elese) of stealing and pocketing money supposedly from the RDP for the building of houses. It was Mrs Ngozi's son, Thembelani, who had been killed in May and her mother a few weeks later at his funeral. These women were angry, in pain and taking the "law" into their own hands alongside their vigilante partners who were also accused of illegal activities on the wrong side of the law.

At this point, the names of those giving evidence at the commission hearings, other than those already named and those in public office at the time, will be withheld in the interests of protecting both their privacy and their safety.

Mrs M described herself as an "ordinary member of the Women's Power Group" who presented with three main concerns, namely;

- The houses that the "council" was building were too small.

- The councillors did not make themselves available to report back to the community and they believed that the councillors were stealing community money.

- No-one had consulted the women or the community on the rent increases.

Mrs M described her attempts to engage council, through councillor Ncate, to table the grievances of the WPG and had called on councillors Elese and Gwayi to attend several meetings. There had also been attempts by Malibongwe Sopangisa (a UMAC - Unrest Monitoring Action Committee - not for profit organisation representative) to organise meetings under his facilitation to avoid violence, which had not occurred because the community hall had been locked.

At any time when the parties had met there had been a lot of conflict between the women of the RDP forum and the WPG and it was after the failure of the meeting on 21st January, 1998 that the WPG had decided on the sit-in at the IKAPA administrative offices in Crossroads.

They had been visited by the secretary for the executive committee of the Cape Town City Council and had given their demands to him, which were for 48 square metre houses. They had also alleged that R5 million had been stolen by the councillors, from the RDP. In addition, there were no services being rendered to their sites so they could not agree to the recent rates increases. They had also asked to meet with the executive committee, the Mayor, Theresa Solomon and the executive committee chair, Nomaindia Mfeketo.

So where did these claims come from? The commission had previously heard from the Director of Housing at the time. We knew that the

Integrated Serviced Land Project, undertaken by the Department of Housing and Planning of the Provincial Administration of the Western Cape (PAWC) involved the development of Phases 3, 4 and 5 of Crossroads.

The Cape Town Municipal Housing Directorate therefore had no direct responsibility for the development project but it was they who were responsible for the approval of the town planning and engineering design. They would have to approve housing plans, provide objections to the Provincial Housing Development Board, provide services, maintain infrastructure and levy rates and service charges. They would also be responsible for the provision and maintenance of community facilities.

Infrastructure development had in fact begun in 1996, having been facilitated by the local RDP forum, eager to get into delivery as soon as possible.

Apparently, an erroneous press release had been issued at this early time in August 1996, giving the newly elected Crossroads councillors an amount of R10 million, initially, with a further R34 million given by the city council to build houses in Phase 3 and Boys Town areas. In fact, the council had already invested R11 million in the cost of infrastructure development in 1994 and there was no money to be had for the building of houses.

So, clearly, the expectations which would have arisen as a result of this huge injection of funds were at odds with the reality. The ISLP director requested the housing director to disabuse the residents through the councillors from their convictions that the council was raking in millions for the building of houses in the community. The councillors were not persuadable and continued to inflate expectations. In the meantime, the real budget set down for the development of houses through the RDP amounted to R17,250 for each house. This was further broken down to R8,750 for the building of infrastructure to service the house with the residue of R8,500 for the actual structural building.

Tenders went out to housing contractors who were invited to construct "show" houses. Three contractors produced 25 square metre houses and one contractor produced a 36 square metre house. It was clear that the previous standard of 42 square metres in Phase 1 was not to be reached and the 36 square metre example was judged as inferior in workmanship. Still, the ISLP project committee insisted that this be on offer and of the first 100 beneficiaries (selected by our completely compromised councillors), 82 chose this house and 18 chose the 25 square metre house. These were to be built by the contractor, Envirex, and were completed by the end of 1997. The contractor, Ms Da Silva, for the 36 square metre houses, completed no houses and handed over her contract to a Mr Patel. He was also unable to deliver to contract and by the end of February 1998, handed over the contract to a Mr Kevin Francis. His contract was to be cancelled by the Provincial Administration of the Western Cape (PAWC) at the end of June, with no fulfilment of its terms but individuals were able to contract directly with Mr Francis if they wished to continue to try and get something done.

This established a great opportunity for contractors who, although they had been approved by the Provincial Housing Development, were to be policed by no-one, hence the infiltration of our vigilante protectionist or rather, extortionist criminals.

In the meantime, the women of the WPG had steadfastly rejected even the elusory 36 square metre houses, holding onto their ideal and originally promised 46 square metre house. Additionally, some 13 of them had refused to be removed from the Section 2 development area to make way for the new houses to be built in Phase 4. These shacks were obstructing the completion of building in Phase 3 with the risk of major cost implications.

Negotiations with the women had proved unsuccessful and PAWC was reluctant to get another court order evicting them which would have to be forceful and inevitably shed more blood. These shacks then became the focus of conflicting party interests and the antagonism resulted in gun battles across this land in the second half of July.

Right about the time we were settling down to the commission hearings.

Mrs M described the burning of houses and the shooting events, the arrests of various youth members, the attempts by the police to arrest the women for trespassing in the IKAPA offices, from February through to the end of July.

She also reported that councillor Ncate, since October 1997, had been promising these women 58 square metre houses. He had stated that the R17,250 was for the building of houses and had not mentioned the infrastructure costs. Neither had councillors Gwayi and Elese ever told them anything to the contrary. In fact, according to Mrs M, there was a clear perception that they had made off with the balance of the funding, leaving them with a very poor third best option of 25 square metre houses.

It is a totally understandable position to take up, one would think.

Mrs K, also a member of the WPG, confirmed these positions exactly. She also provided some light on the reasons why the meetings which the councillors swore they had convened, were not attended - because they had been held in parts of Crossroads inaccessible to the WPG late at night, where, because of their political allegiances to the old

CONTRALESA warlords, Nongwe, Nxobongwana, Toise, etc. they were at real risk from attack by supporters of the new political leadership (councillors).

She also pointed to the fact that many of the WPG had indeed lost their homes and were now forced to live at the council offices for protection. They were protected by the Qibla youth and affiliated APLA youth. (As already described, PAGAD, the People Against Gangsterism and Drugs, had already declined into a motley crew of gangsters and were by now openly supported by the radical Muslim group, Qibla, of Cape Town, hence the name of the youth group "protecting " the WPG.) PAGAD was by this time in open defiance with state police forces and whilst the state tried to pin criminal violence charges onto PAGAD from 1997 onwards, they were unsuccessful until 2000. Allegations of police infiltration from gangs were rife and yet again these rumours could not be taken lightly, given the past history with the "third force" and the "witdoeke."

Not surprisingly, as the commission progressed in listening to the women of the WPG, these stories were repeated again and again.

CHAPTER 7

THE PERSONALITIES

Chapter 7

THE PERSONALITIES

Director Mpembe, the newly appointed Commissioner of Police for the Crossroads and Philippi areas, was also to give witness to the commission. He presented as a tall, strong, quietly spoken individual who was thoughtful in his responses and who, having only recently been appointed to this role, had clearly taken time to try and understand the circumstances surrounding the anarchy he had inherited. He had an open face and his management of both the commission hearings (and our numerous calls to him for support, guidance and escort through the townships) and his team of scared policemen, was to build an enormous amount of respect among us as we progressed. At the time, this man would have to have been a hero to have undertaken the Herculean task of leading his team back to strong policing in a community where they were naturally hated, often with due cause. Either he was courageous or bloody stupid.

We were to learn from our dealings with him, that he was in no way stupid but rather, that he was driven by a strong sense of natural justice and the will to make things right. It was Director Mpembe who would peel back the layers of the criminal justice system for us so that we could understand exactly why the work we were doing was so important, why there was no way the system was going to be able to cope with the truth at all and that our findings of corruption extended all the way from the criminal gutters to the highest arms of local justice.

From the beginning of the year it had become well reported that the police investigation and preparation of criminal cases were both incompetent and negligent. The question was, was this a case of negligent omission or was there something much more pervasive like corruption going on?

A good example of this was the case of Victor Sam, a Crossroads warlord and a taxi strongman – leader of the Cape Amalgamated Taxi Association (CATA). He'd been arrested for shooting three men in their knees in Gugulethu– in an Irish Republican Army-like attack. He'd been arrested and charged several times before for murder and kidnapping but had so far avoided being convicted. In 1995 he'd been acquitted on 21 charges including murder and attempted murder. A month later, charges for the kidnapping of two men and their consequent murder were also withdrawn and this was 3 days after he had been granted R4,000 bail on another murder charge. Unbelievable as it seems, he appeared to be untouchable. He clearly had the funds to hire his legal representation and meet his bail payments. Then there was the police admission that witnesses could not be induced to testify, even with an offer of reward, as they feared for their lives.

When he walked into office on the 14th of April 1998, Director Mpembe was inheriting a very complex problem. At the time, his predecessor, Acting Director Perry had handed the responsibility of the WPG sit–in and consequent retaliatory action groups like the "pro-Crossroads development constituency" - primarily from the local RDP forum, to the Cape Town City Council and the ANC, as "the police did not want to be seen to be taking sides." In the meantime, clashes between the WPG and their protectors, the "Qibla"/APLA youth groups, the comrades of the ANC youth and the intimidation of the developers and builders on site in Phase 3 and 4 of the housing developments continued unabated. The police force themselves seemed both emasculated and corrupt.

On the 16th of April, five or six WPG members had been arrested and an interdict restraining the women from interfering in the development process had been issued by the Mitchell's Plain Magistrate's Courts. On the 17th, infrastructure development had recommenced in Phase 3. On 21st April in a "search and seizure" raid, five firearms were confiscated from a PAC training room and meeting place. On the 24th April, Mpembe announced that both police and South African Defence Force (SANDF) patrols would increase as a result of a dreadful month giving rise to twelve shacks being burned down and 14 people being injured, some of them having been involved in attempted murders, both protagonists and victims.

It was Mpembe who came out clearly accusing Jeffrey Nongwe, now the head of a known CATA hit squad, of covertly driving the anti–development faction in the conflict, with the support of the APLA youth. The pro-development group, led by councillors Elese and Gwayi, had been retaliating. Essentially, out of all the mess, Ngxobongwana and Nongwe wanted to be both councillors and warlords who could continue to reap the rewards of rental payments for their established informal settlements, at the expense of the rates and services to the council for the formal development sites. So they were boycotting all development and the spiralling violence was mobilising the mass community support in the build-up to the 1999 elections.

By taking firm control, Mpembe initially commanded respect from both faction sides. He had attended a community workshop facilitated by UMAC, with the participation of all faction groups including the Community Policing Forums, the local RDP forums from Nyanga, Crossroads, and Philippi East (Brown's Farm), correctional services, the Mitchell's Plain Magistrate's Court, social welfare services, SANCO, WECUSA and CRORA. Violence and gangsterism were the two main agenda items and the Nyanga Community Safety Forum was launched with the commitment of the PAC and WPG constituencies.

However, the spiral continued and, as previously reported, by the time the commission started its work in July there were 10 cases of murder, 40 arson cases and 21 attempted murder cases, amongst others of a less serious nature. Whilst there had been a lull in the pace of violence and an embrace of a better world vision, the perpetrators continued to be bailed with ease and there could be no respect for the law as charges were not "sticking."

When he appeared before the commission, Mpembe cited the dire resources needed for his police force. The Unathi Village satellite station had been closed in 1996 "due to the violence" and of the 32 vehicles in his jurisdiction, most were in for repair. (You will recall that access and road services within both Crossroads and Philippi was very close to impossible). He stated that he needed at least 50 vehicles in full operational order.

He also stated that whilst there had been no systematic approach to reporting and recording of information since 1993, he had instituted proper incident reporting in the two months since his appointment. Astoundingly, this meant that the current stats on murder, arson, attempted murder and the like were in all likelihood severely underreported! He had only 6 investigators but needed ten to "trace suspects and to ensure that they were detained without bail."

He came across as committed to social engagement through the building of relationships across all community groups and had initiated social upliftment programmes to bring about social change.

He understood that there was a need for democratisation, to move away from the traditional leaders like Nongwe and Ngxobongwana and that the community would have to face the inevitable rejection of this idea from these warlords who would lose their traditional income sources.

He identified political rivalry between the parties in the lead up to the elections, acknowledging that they would be a catalyst for further violence.

Mpembe also identified the criminal elements that had crept into the foray through the Taxi Association's wars, through the PAGAD relationships to "Qibla" and their APLA associations etc. and shared the intelligence reports he was able to access from national intelligence services. As the commission hearings progressed, we were to become alarmed at the number of arms being confiscated in Mpembe's raids and were to follow the bad smell to its source. More on this later.

Let's have a look at the councillors.

In late October 1998, Toise, a warlord who had previously terrorised the Philippi East community, was arrested whilst trying to return to residence there (amidst strong violent resistance). Another known criminal, Siyabulela Khoba had been arrested on seventeen charges, two of which were for murder. Both had been released on bail, which had been secured by an advocate who had previously served as a magistrate at the Mitchell's Plain Magistrates Court. Councillor Elese and his supporters had publicly backed this move and it was alleged that he was behind the violence being perpetrated by Khobo and councillor Gwayi's two sons. Councillor Gwayi's sons, wanted by the police for their transgressions, were allegedly driving taxis in Langa at the time. It was also alleged that councillor Ncate was driving Khobo to and from court hearings.

These councillors had also allegedly been trying to (unconstitutionally) undermine and dissolve the Community Policing Forum in Crossroads. In November, sadly, the Community Policing Forum established shortly after Mpembe's appointment, failed to keep its meeting commitments, thus dashing the hopes raised at its inception for an inclusive, solution finding body.

Mpembe also reported to the commission that CATA taxis had been seen patrolling the roads in Crossroads at night, leading to the conclusion that this was the work of the old traditional alliances. Wrong again. Our friend, Victor Sam, had reportedly withdrawn his support of Jeffrey Nongwe and was now closely aligned with our councillors, Gwayi and Elese. What was his interest in the development programme? Well he was demanding that a butchery and a garage be built for him in exchange for his "protection." All in all, there had been eighty two (82) charges brought against Victor Sam and none had been proven – no witnesses. The taxi wars were back on the boil again, disputation flaring between the CATA and Mitchell's Plain taxis.

In their submissions to the commission, councillors Ncate, Gwayi and Elese's statements were fairly indistinguishable from each other. They all dismissed the WPG members as troublemakers, rude and obnoxious. They all considered themselves as honest, hardworking and humble. They all considered that director Mpembe was acting without a mandate from the community. Ncate was so out of touch with the facts of the development programme that even in the commission hearings he insisted that the houses being built were all 36 square metres and further, that Kevin Francis the contractor was going to build 500 houses of 54, 46 and 36 square metres. He denied that the councillors were in any way responsible for the allocation of houses and on the causes of violence, he pointed to the UDM (United Democratic Movement), a new political party trying to build a support base, as the instigator.

Depoutch "Whitey" Elese, born in Ugie in the Eastern Cape, arrived in the Western Cape in 1979 and joined the ANC in the early 80s. He signed up for the armed wing, uMkhonto we Siswe in 1985. In 1989 he was involved in the youth recruitment in schools from their student representative councils and in 1990 was elected chair of the Unathi Branch of the ANC. He joined the National Peacekeeping Force in the transition years, between 1990 and 1994 and then with the inauguration of President Mandela, was integrated into the South African Defence Force as were many others. In 1995 he was called by the ANC to stand as a councillor for Crossroads and subsequent to his landslide election he resigned from the SANDF in 1996.

As part of the RDP Forum, the elected councillors had placed out to tender the infrastructure development plan for Phase 4 in Crossroads at that time.

Nongwe and other members of the PAC had complained to the provincial administration that they had not been part of the election for the RDP forum and were therefore not consulted on the development plan. This had been denied by members of the Integrated Serviced Land Project who claimed that Nongwe and his counterparts were part of the election, they had just not been elected.

Elese had demonstrated a clear understanding of the subsidy of R17,250, the cost of the infrastructure at R8,750 and the balance of R8,500 to be used for the construction of the houses. Up until this point his story concurred exactly with that of the development team at council, previously explained. He just had not bothered to get this message across to his electorate.

His explanation as to how houses were chosen and allocated was slightly different from that presented to the commission by others. He said that 110 people from Section 2 signed up for houses and that priority had been given to those who had lived there for 22 years or more. (He had only been in the Western Cape for 19 years at that time.)

When asked why he had made no attempt to talk to his constituents and to clarify any residual misunderstandings, he gave the excuse that he had referred matters to councillor Gwayi as he had been incapacitated through a motor vehicle accident and because of his cast could not attend meetings, specifically the meeting of 21st January.

However, the ANC executive had clearly felt differently because they had collected him on the 25th January and driven him to a meeting with the WPG to clarify claims that he had failed to consult with them on service charges, amongst others. He stated that he believed that he had done this well enough. He had also called upon ANC members of the WPG to excuse themselves from the group which he explained did not enjoy a "locus standi" with any of the other groups involved in the sit-in. He reported that the WPG were rude, abusive and had thrown stones at him, just as they had at the mayor, and the Exco Chair.

Quite how he reconciled his easy explanation of rates charges and his failure to consult with a group of assailants in full flight is a little difficult to understand. Construction of infrastructure and houses had been blockaded from this point until a meeting called in March and requested by the newly appointed Director Mpembe. Elese was of the opinion, so he stated, that the majority of those in attendance at this meeting were in support of continued development. He accused those who were against it as being from Unathi, (unfortunately not from his original area of Ugie) and who already had houses. Consequent to this meeting, supported by unemployed members of the community who went out to the sites to protect the developers, the programme was reignited.

Elese had described attacks on members of his party during April. He was rightly fearful for his life as he had been ambushed by eight individuals, one of whom he identified as Thembelani Ngozi (murdered in the following month) and others associated with the WPG and Contralesa. Elese had barely escaped this attack and explained that he had been party to an ANC initiative to infiltrate the PAC camps whereby they had been able to inform the police of huge arms stashes. This had initially resulted in six arrests and consequent to a similar attack on councillor Gwayi's home, another eight arrests. Heavy weapons, R4, R1, G3, 303's and R5 rifles had been seized together with hand grenades. The big question was, where were these weapons coming from? They were defence force and police issue!

Elese described Johnson Ngxobongwana's visitations to the WPG sit-in and how he provided food and support to them. On being asked why the PAC would align themselves with a man of this ilk, as a member of the National Party, Elese's response was that the Clarence Makwetu "camp" divided from the Dr. Magobo "camp" of the PAC was supplying Ngxobongwana with weapons through the APLA forces.

On being asked why, Elese stated that this was because the ANC had promised schools, parks, clinics, jobs and houses. This would have detracted from Ngxobongwana's popularity as a traditionalist leader. He also stated that Patricia de Lille (then mayor of Cape Town) and the head of the PAC had met with PAGAD and together, the PAC and PAGAD, were supplying food and support to the WPG sit-in.

This was apparently being managed by Eliot Gxokwe, a PAC member in the area. He was arrested in 1992 and sentenced to 17 years imprisonment but released prior to the elections in 1994. He was now a gunman for Ngxobongwana.

As chairman of Contralesa, Jeffrey Nongwe and Johnson Ngxobongwana had buried their differences and both were seen as major collaborators behind the WPG. An interesting insight given by Elese was his acknowledgement that if the women's issues with the size of the houses was dealt with, this would significantly corrode Ngxobongwana and Nongwe's power base. Well, yes!

Elese went on to deal with his and Ncate's bail applications for known criminals as a right in their personal capacities and not as members of council. He denied any allegation of corruption as he was not personally involved in any housing allocation. He responded to questions concerning his engagement and consultation by stating that he was covering his obligations in that regard by reporting back to the RDP forum and to his own committee.

He was to reappear before the commission on 6th October to respond to questions about his involvement in the shootings and murder at Thembelani Ngozi's funeral. He claimed that the first time he heard that he was alleged to have been involved in this was on this day, 6th October, and never before. He had an alibi and a raft of witnesses to back up his story, mainly pointing to the APLA intimidation of taxis near and around his house on the day of the funeral.

He also said that the goat that he had slaughtered the day before Thembelani's funeral and the party he was having on the day itself had nothing to do with Thembelani's death, but was just a family celebration.

He was called upon to answer numerous other claims which had now surfaced regarding his nepotism in the appointment of people with whom he was closely affiliated, to key jobs in the council in the area; all of which he refuted.

He also dismissed the conflict between himself and the ANC Buntubakhe Branch as sour grapes in the fallout from his landslide victory in the elections and that there had been no irregularities in the voting process.

He denied any knowledge of any of the violent attacks on any of his opponents in the Buntubakhe Branch of the RDP, although he admitted to there being very strained relationships with those under attack.

He admitted at this hearing that there had been no meetings for report back to any constituents of the Buntubakhe Branch of the RDP.

He acknowledged that whilst he was quite happy to meet with the executives of local structures aligned with his development plans, he would only meet with those not aligned at a later date.

Councillor Melford Gwayi also concurred with the funding allocation for the cost of infrastructure and houses to be built. He also confirmed the tendering process and the choices given to community members eligible for housing. He had, in fact, met with founding members of the WPG as far back as October 1997, when they had clearly laid out their grievances, including allegations of misappropriation of funds. He states that some of their problems related to Ward 18, not his ward but that of Elese and he had pointed to him for resolution. His ward was apparently happy for the development to go ahead.

Strikingly clear to the commission was that this councillor truly believed matters to be much simpler than we had been led to believe thus far. There were only problems in other people's jurisdictions, not his. Unfortunately, given the level of violent consequence for many of the players, he could not have been anything but naïve at best but most likely deliberately messing with the truth.

Like Elese, there was a lot less than the candour we required to get to the bottom of the story. His depiction of the WPG was entirely different. They were expecting much bigger houses because they had been promised them, they wanted clean schools and clean clinics and the reopening of a crèche in their area. In order to support these needs they had decided to boycott any attempts made to develop anything.

The fact that he had been arrested and detained for arson and shooting attacks, killing two people on 29th June, was dealt with by simply denying that he had any involvement with any violence at all. He was out on bail after all.

One of the killings involved his own brother-in-law, Mr Tom, who supported the WPG.

Bail for this case had been set at R2,000.

One case had subsequently been dismissed and the other two, he said he "was not worried about as the charges were false" and he had alibi's in both instances.

Bail for these, the shooting and arson charges, had been set at R1,000.

The charges had been laid because the WPG did not want him to be a councillor any more.

Absurd as these accounts are, (and one could not make them up, they are so bizarre), this is what we were contending with and somehow we were expected to make head and tail sense of it all and bring it together in a picture which could be seen, touched, understood and managed. It was becoming increasingly unclear as to how this would be achieved.

CHAPTER 8

THE COMMISSION

Chapter 8

THE COMMISSION

We were to convene commission hearings for fifteen sittings from 16th July until 14th November. All were public hearings which were well advertised and clearly communicated. There were only three witness accounts held in camera due to the sensitivity of the information we were being given. These were;

- The Crossroads Community Police Forum Task Team;
- A Superintendent of the South African Police Force; and
- An individual witness.

The media was in attendance for many of our sessions.

We also received 16 written submissions from individuals and organisations active in the areas during the period of review.

All of our hearings were recorded and transcripts typed of the submissions made. As commissioners, we could ask questions of witnesses and probe evidence but as we were not a court of law, statements were not made under oath. Witnesses were simply asked to say that they spoke the truth – clearly with no great success on many counts.

Due to the sensitivity and volatility of the process, armed security was deployed for the duration of the commission and guarded transport was provided for the witnesses, interest parties and anyone who wished to observe the process.

Whilst we originally convened at the Athlone Civic Centre we were asked to move to the Cape Town Civic Centre by our security as they had received advice, just before our fourth sitting on 15th August, 1998, that there were attacks planned on the Athlone Centre. We were not sure exactly who was making the plans but we were absolutely sure that they were likely to be carried out.

In the initial hearings I had settled into my role quite comfortably, focusing on any and every opportunity to build bridges from a conflict management and design point of view. As chair, Essa Moosa was ably leading us into each witness examination with skill and expertise and the transcription process was working well. Our secretariat was doing a marvellous job with logistical planning and co-ordination and we seemed to be able to manage all party's needs for separation, isolation, privacy and grandstanding. Bulelwa Tinto, together with Mlamli Mfenyana were invaluable in assisting us with translations from mostly Xhosa and Zulu languages, both written and oral statements and from an events management perspective it was all going as smoothly as could be expected…until the rainbow once again dissolved.

At around the fifth hearing there was great news that Essa Moosa, our chair, had been appointed to the Supreme Court of South Africa as an Acting Judge. The bad news was that the appointment was in Bloemfontein, in the Free State.

As he broke the news to us, it slowly dawned upon my naïve self that whilst he promised to try and attend most of the remaining hearings, he would not be around for a lot of the 'behind the scenes' work in digesting the evidence and coming up with the findings which would lead us to the recommendations, all of which was called for in our contract. At that point, it had become clear to us all that because Mlamli Mfenyana lived within the community he would be placing himself at great risk to do this work and it was difficult for him to get to places at night when this work was being done. I was deeply aware of a sense of creeping despair as I realised that the responsibility of writing this report would fall onto my shoulders.

At no point should anyone think that either Essa or Mlamli were shirking responsibility, it was not like that at all, but rather the culmination of circumstances which came crashing down upon me at a time when I was least expecting it. This was exactly what I had so desperately tried to avoid, given the increasing responsibility of growing a new business and a young family. But what to do? There was no alternative and no reasonably decent nor honourable way of extrication.

My biggest concern from that point was to ensure that I managed the collation of material evidence, the transcripts and the translations as tightly as possible and whilst I had good access to Essa via phone conversations, I had to bring in a few of my own resources to support the project. Obviously, it was essential to maintain the integrity of the information and to reflect this with the greatest accuracy possible.

So, from one hearing to the next, some with the presence and support of both of my fellow commissioners, sometimes with just me and Mlamli, there was a team of people working with our secretariat, Bulelwa and Jongi, on translations, transcriptions and then supporting me with interpretation and distillation of the truth.

Most significantly, as we came to the close of November 1998, our business personal assistant, Kate, who lived in Fish Hoek at the time, would go home to her family at around five in the evening and then be back at my home office at around eight to begin a mammoth work session of the commission report with me until three in the morning. Occasionally, my business partners Steve Woods and Terry Murphy, who would often stay with me when he was travelling from the UK, would read through the first drafts of the report and give me suggested edits to try and make a little more sense to the reader, of the complexities which were so overwhelming for me at the time. I shall remain forever indebted to them for their sacrifices as we were all so often emotionally overwrought by the evidence given by some of the victims of violence.

Sadly, having given up smoking when I was pregnant with my daughter in 1997, I was back on the smokes again, having succumbed weakly to the perceived escape they would give me from the horrible information we were having to deal with. As Kate was a smoker too, we'd sit in this dark, lamplit office, knowing that we had a beautiful view over the whole of False Bay in front of us, shrouded in clouds of smoke. My method was to read the transcripts, form a reference point on each one, reframe it to reflect the evidence on a tape recorder. Kate then transcribed this, working with headphones as she typed onto her computer. She'd have to put up with my sobbing as I tried to understand how people survived the trauma they had suffered, then break down herself as she transcribed it. I recall one evening when Terry was reading a draft and having him break down into racking sobs as he read the transcript, a man of the world who could not understand the depravity and cruelty of our human race.

At times like this there was a lot of wine consumed as we came to the end of a late session, whilst we put ourselves back together to face another day. It was a time of living in the twilight of reality.

In my suburban white world of privilege, in beautiful Cape Town, there was a successful business, a beautiful home, a wonderful little family complete with thriving children and happy, tail-wagging dogs to complement the picture. It was a world of the rainbow, of hope and sunlight and aspiration for everything to settle and work well for everyone.

In my night-time world it was lonely, dark, shrouded by evil and consumed by conspiracies of history. It was unbelievable for most of the time and it was only in late September as the report began to take its final shape, that Dave, my husband asked me whether it would have any impact on our lives. I was glib in my answer at first. I had never felt unsafe for myself, as I had been in sticky situations before, and so naturally assumed that my work profile would once again protect me from anyone taking my assessment personally. But then I clearly had not thought about the impact the assessment would have on murderers, arsonists, rapists and bullies.

CHAPTER 9

THE QUESTIONS WE WERE BEING ASKED TO ANSWER.

Chapter 9

THE QUESTIONS WE WERE BEING ASKED TO ANSWER.

Who could be trusted to tell the truth? To be honest, the only people the commission grew to trust were the third party non-governmental organisations who were trying to broker the peace between all the warring factions.

So who was at war with whom and who was in bed with whom?

In the commission's view, there were ten different interest groups directly involved in the conflict. These included;

- The Cape Town City Councillors – all of whom were ANC members and through them their associated armed "comrades" youth groups. The councillors were also specifically linked with Victor Sam and his armed taxi heavies.

- The Political Parties – the ANC and the PAC being the predominantly active parties, with the associated presence of the IFP, NP and the UDM.

- The Warlords – Ngzobongwana, Nongwe, Toise (in Philippi) and their associated headmen. They, through their associations with the "third force" and "witdoeke" gangs and through them to the police activities under the apartheid regime were particularly scary.

- The Police – with the significant distinction of the newly appointed Director Mpembe separated from his police force, as yet unidentified individually into trustworthy/untrustworthy groups.

- The Public Prosecutor's office – those attorneys supposedly serving the people, there to apply the law and see to it that the people were protected and who were so remarkably unsuccessful at their task.

- The Magistrate's Court judges themselves, at higher office, allowing bail and release applications at ridiculously low costs to those repeat offenders charged with murder, arson, property destruction, intimidation and the like.

- The Women's Power Group – a group which clearly started out with a multi-party membership, including ANC and PAC members, but which evolved to be regarded as partisan to the warlords, the PAC specifically, PAGAD and their armed fundamentalist "Qibla Youth."

- The Cape Town City Council and all it's officials - under the ANC party majority.

- The Provincial Administration - under the National Party majority.

- The civic organisations - all of whom seemed to be politically and therefore faction aligned. So the local RDP Forums, aligned to the ANC and therefore the councillors, and the WECUSA breakaway CRORA group aligned to the traditional leaders, who seemed unable to stick to any party political hat when

> the party did not support them. So Ngzobongwana, ANC, then 'turned' to NP and Nongwe, ANC to Independent candidate, both hated each other and fought each other for territory, later joined forces and both linked to the PAC through their clear and partial support for the WPG.

The first group, the councillors, we know were accused of a number of things. First and foremost, the commission found that there were deep concerns in the community that;

- they were not communicating, or giving feedback, or consulting with the entire community either accurately or fully enough and

- when communication did occur, it was not necessarily bound by truth but had indeed inspired unrealistic expectations which had exacerbated a very difficult situation for the Cape Town City Council

- the councillors saw themselves as leading only their interest groups in the community, therefore as political leaders and not as community leaders responsible for local government and

- they abused their council positions by being involved in the selection process for employee applicants to council, favouring family and friends

- they were allied to criminal groups.

With regard to political party conflict, there was clearly inter-party conflict between the different parties and some unholy alliances already discussed. Within the parties themselves, there was also conflict. For example, intra-party conflict within the PAC, (the Clarence Makweto Group and the Doctor Magobo Group) and within the ANC between the Buntubakhe branch of the ANC and the ANC councillors themselves, especially Depoutch Elese. Again, the political party mantles had alliances with criminal groups driving the methods in which disputes were being managed. PAGAD and APLA/'Qibla' youth, gangs of youths who had previously identified themselves as "self defence units" /SDUs retaliating against the "third force" active during the apartheid years. These groups, with little or no policing in the area, were resurrected and now settling old scores, always with the innocents in the middle.

Amidst the confusion in public leadership, the warlords, the traditional leadership, were at war with each other, with and between their respective headmen, and certainly with any attempt to establish any law and order in the townships where their income was derived from the terrified residents.

We know that Director Mbembe was genuinely trying to deal with the issues but a lack of capacity in the resources available to him, the void in trust between the police themselves and the community they served, conspired against him to render his attempts ineffective in the overall picture of growing violence.

The Cape Town City Council, unable to deliver services to the community and unable to ensure clarity in its communication through the councillors to the community was itself rendered ineffectual. The relationship between it and the Provincial Administration, the management of the funding supply, the distribution of funds and the accounting of disbursements remained a mystery. It is no wonder that amidst claims of corruption all round, it was hard to believe that the alternative, a clean balance sheet was the truth and to be believed. Councillors, especially Ncate's relationship with the ISLP and his relationships with the developing contracts would have engendered the not unreasonable assumption that there was something amiss, especially when the promised bigger houses were not being delivered. The councillor's consequent unavailability to meet with concerned citizens only served to reinforce those suspicions.

In answer to the questions above, everyone was at war with everyone, there were a lot of really strange bedfellows and aside from a marginal few, no-one could be trusted.

Imagine what it was like to live in this world.

Victim after victim came to talk to the commission about their horrendous experiences in Crossroads and Philippi. They would tell of nights of terror when armed groups would invade their homes and only if they were lucky, would they be allowed to leave with their lives intact. More often than not, members of their families were murdered in front of them, women were kidnapped only to return later, raped and traumatised and children were sometimes victims and witnesses of these crimes. Houses, with all their meagre possessions were burned down.

Consequently, there was a crisis in the local schools. Because of the volatility, children were often not able to attend school. Learning for children who had been traumatised was extremely difficult and absenteeism rocketed. Discipline within the schools had been destroyed, with children becoming aggressive and behaviours manifesting in assault against teachers a common occurrence.

Omar Valley, who at the time was the head of the United Nations Safer Cities programme, stated that as many as 50% of the violent crimes were going unreported. Of those that were reported we know that in less than 50% of the cases were there any arrests being made and of these, if charges were laid, the chances of a perpetrator ever being brought to trial were minimal. They either escaped, or were allowed disgracefully achievable bail applications, often supported by political leadership. If the charges were laid, the courts deliberated, then the likelihood of a stringent sentence fit to punish the crime was highly doubtful, with the perpetrators most likely to return within a short period of time. If that happened, then the chances of retribution were high.

It was no wonder that the victims preferred to remain silent.

This brings me to why I write this story. It is for the silent voices who trusted us with the truth, who came, despite the very real threat to themselves, because someone had to listen, someone had to hear, someone had to care. The tipping point came for me, when in late September, the story of a massacre in a home in the townships came to the commission.

A mother and child clinging to her skirt, hiding from anyone who approached, came to make a statement. Essa Moosa was not present on that day so I was chairing the hearings and there were the usual flurries of different observer groups trying to establish their space and status inside the commission rooms.

Having made her statement to tell the truth, she began by telling us the history surrounding her story. She had made a police statement approximately thee months beforehand giving witness to an event whereby she had seen a group of men enter a neighbour's house, throw everyone out having shot one of the residents and then leave having torched the house, which burned down completely. She had identified two of the perpetrators whom she had recognised and charges had been laid at the police station as a consequence.

On the day her world turned upside down she had been in her own house, together with members of her family. A neighbour had shouted an alert to her that there was a group approaching her house and that they looked threatening.

Knowing the risk to her family, she had run to her neighbour's house to call the police as she had been told to do and begged them to come to her aid. The men had in the meantime entered her house and there was a lot of shouting and screaming and gunshots to be heard. She ran screaming back to her house to find that her family had all been killed. This included her mother, her sister and all of her children, or so she thought initially. The men had taken her outside the house and then made her watch as they cut the throat of her eleven year old son. The message to her was that this was her reward for giving evidence against members of their gang. They had left her absolutely and appallingly devastated on the bloodied steps of her home.

She was later to discover her four year old daughter had climbed beneath the couch and so had avoided her own demise but this little girl, who appeared with her mother at the commission, was completely mute. She had not spoken a word since the day of the massacre.

I cannot write this story, nor tell it to anyone without it bringing up the most overwhelming sense of despair and loss that was palpable throughout the hearings on that day. What could one say to someone who had lost so much, who had witnessed so much evil, who continued to watch her daughter suffer so much trauma? How could we offer any consolation to one who must have been in such despair?

I cried for days after this hearing. Together, my PA and I cried as we wrote up the transcripts, as we formulated response statements for the findings report and my partners cried as they read through the edits.

It was and will always be the worst kind of story in the most ghastly framework of terror I can think of.

Yet this woman had the courage to come to the commission to tell her story. In a public forum, in front of others, in defiance of the very evil which had destroyed her life. She told me that she did so for her daughter, as one day she hoped that her daughter would find her voice again, that she could begin a new life in a world where there was real law and order, where there was hope for a better life.

Against all of the repeated stories of violence which we had heard, it is this one which has remained with me for all these years.

CHAPTER 10

HORROR

Chapter 10

HORROR

These are direct transcripts of some of the stories which should always remind us why we are so lucky to be living in circumstances where our basic human rights are respected and guaranteed. (Names changed for their safety.)

Lindiwe – On the 19th June this year on Friday, we were in the house (we were seven), having supper. There was a knock at the door and we let him in. Once inside the guy fired shots and killed four of my relatives and three of us survived. We called the police and ambulance. The person I recognised as the one who shot me by the name of XXXX. He fired four shots and I was taken to Groote Schuur Hospital.

Nongwe - On Thursday something to 8pm I walked from the station with Mr. M I saw these four and others I cannot identify. Around 10pm they fired shots and one of them hit me in the shoulder and I was helped by Mr. M as he kept me tight on the ground. There are ten bullet holes in my house. Mr. M was shot in his arm. The police arrived and took me to hospital. Now my right arm is not working and I am breathing with the pipe now. I am even unable to make a living and I am self employed. It is very hard and I have five children depending solely on me and we have no food now at all.

Abigail – My father was shot dead on 24th April this year by these four. The person who entered the house was XXXX who shot my dad. XXXX stood at the door and XXXX stood next to the toilet. They were arrested but XXXX is out on bail. The problem I have with my boy now is that he cannot go to school properly and since he was beaten by (the one who is out on bail) he has a problem with his ear. My son requires witness protection services and counselling. I have five children, all dependents of mine and I am not working.

Nomonde – During the month of May this year I was going with Lindi in the area of XXXX. He came out of his room and insulted and threatened to kill me. Some time later he came to my house with XXXX and three policemen demanding to search claiming that there are weapons. My husband let them do their job but they got nothing because there were no weapons. The reason why he insulted me was that I asked whether they are police or what. I said to him and his friend that they must leave my house. I went and reported the matter to the Lower Crossroads police station but nothing was done.

Sandile – On the 15th June 1998, Thandi came to me saying that XXXX's place was on fire. When we arrived there the house was already burned including XXXX's brother (smaller) who died in the house. On the 24th June 1998, I saw these (eight) kicking doors and breaking windows taking things out of my house which includes TV, 2 burner stoves, bed, hi-fi speakers and the door of the fridge was broken and the toilet where I kept my dishes (hiding these dishes) were taken away with them. I asked the police to accompany me to establish the damage caused and we went back to the charge office to lay a charge. So since then we never had any rest.

Patience – I am a resident of Browns farm and I have three children. I have a title deed. I was chased away by people who do not have sites. Since 1993 my house was burned down. Mr XXXX was still alive at the time. He and (two others) belonged to the same click that was committing all these crimes. Even now I am not staying there and all my belongings were burned.
Albert – On 27th April 1998, while I was fixing my car, XXXX came and shot at me and my car windscreen. I was hospitalised. In my discharge from hospital, I laid a charge. Until now, XXXX has not been arrested.

Beauty – On 16th June I was evicted from my house in a very bad manner. I was kicked out by three young men and I left all my belongings. On the following day they came back and I was not there. They demolished my house. My 24-year-old child was also kicked out. In the process they were firing shots and I went and reported the matter to the police on several days. They told me that they were not going to attend that incident. The reason behind this is that we do not have money to bribe them. Another most important point is I left my work because my life is at stake. My children do not have something to eat and they are unable to go to school and I do not have a husband.

Margaret – My five roomed house was set on fire with all its contents like bedroom furniture costing R5,000, stoves, tape recorder, my clothes and children's clothing. I don't know how my children will go to school without a uniform or any kind of clothing. I have 5 kids.

Reuben – In the month of July this year on Saturday round about seven in the afternoon, we were in my next door neighbour's house when we heard shots and I was hit at my waist, bums and the knee and (friend) was shot too. I was then rushed to Groote Schuur Hospital and when I came out I was banished and just heard from my daughter that she has asked some people to take care of my house. Still, on that process, I heard that those people were burned by petrol but fortunately they escaped but my house was burned down and my belongings. I have never got anything since I was in hospital and my daughter was intimidated and told that I will never stay there again. It is even hard to go to work because they wait for us along the way to the station. The reason for that I do not know on my side. I would like to be told by them.

Patrick – On 26th June XXXX shot at us. My grandfather was struck by the bullet. They took my bungalow with my clothes and I was left with these that I have on. My bed, TV set and hi-fi system was taken away. My plea is for the removal of the perpetrators of this violence so that peace can be restored. I can't even go to work because of the fear to be shot.

It went on and on and always the same story, the attack, the murder, the burning, the theft and/destruction of meagre possessions, followed by the continuing intimidation and threat to safety. Depositions and statements made in the hearings all carried the same message with dreadful monotony.

CHAPTER 11

HOPE

Chapter 11

HOPE

In late September 1998, I was beginning to pull the formatting of the commission report together in draft. It would go through several edits before final presentation to the council but it was already clear that I would have to write the bulk of it. It was at this time that my husband Dave came to ask me if I was sure that this work was going to be safe for us as a family. This was after I had told him the massacre story and he was now really concerned that our family was going to be put in the firing line. At the time I was very reassuring as I was not convinced that there was any threat to us in comfortable St. James but his question began to play on my mind.

There were options on how the story could be written. A read of the terms of reference would allow for a very esoteric commitment to fact. For example, in identifying the causes of violence one did not necessarily have to identify the perpetrators by personal identity. It could have been written on the basis of groups, alliances, key drivers of dissatisfaction but the mother and child kept me awake at night and it became apparent that the more deeply we explored the evidence, we would serve no lasting purpose or good if we skated across the facts as we saw them emerging.

So we identified the perpetrators, we named them and we stated the allegations for which they could have and should have stood up against in a criminal justice system worth its stature. In this one tiny little way, it felt that we were at least honouring the courage of those who came to bear witness. It was one way of trying to instil some hope that their terrible experiences and their unbelievably tragic losses could be honoured in a formal way, acknowledging them in a record.

In truth there is hope, in justice there is affirmation and only in the telling of the truth is there any hope of forgiveness.

In 1993, (Act number 200), the Interim Constitution of South Africa, under the title of "National Unity and Reconciliation states;"

> "This Constitution provides a historic bridge between the past of a deeply divided society characterised by strife, conflict, untold suffering and injustice and a future founded on the recognition of human rights, democracy and peaceful co-existence and development opportunities for all South Africans, irrespective of colour, race, class, belief or sex. The pursuit of national unity, the wellbeing of all South African citizens and peace requires reconciliation between the people of South Africa and the reconstruction of society.
>
> The adoption of this Constitution lays the secure foundation for the people of South Africa to transcend the divisions of strife in the past which generated gross violations of human rights, the transgression of humanitarian principles in violent conflicts and the legacy of hatred, fear, guilt and revenge. These can now be addressed on the basis that there is a need for understanding but not vengeance, a need for reparation, but not for retaliation, a need for ubuntu* but not for victimisation.

> In order to advance such reconciliation and reconstruction, amnesty shall be granted in respect of acts, omissions and offences associated with political objectives and committed in the course of conflicts of the past…"

The Truth and Reconciliation Commission in South Africa, founded on the above aspirational principle and under the loving and passionate guidance of Archbishop Desmond Tutu, was based on very clear moral dictums, which were undisputedly good. Foundational to its success would be the commitment to total truth and transparency between victim and perpetrator.

Put another way, the principle was that a total commitment to truth, allowing for a public acknowledgement and recognition of the atrocities, would also allow for the building of the bridges towards forgiveness and ultimately toward reconciliation. It was a lofty goal and one which carried so much risk. What could have happened if, in facing the truth, the facts were so appalling and the frailty of human nature so raw, that retribution was the only inevitable result? Therein lies the risk and one of the most significant and brave acts in mankind's history, which I think has not been recognised for its significance in our emerging world.

In the South African context, this commission saw men and women, perpetrators and victims, weeping as the truth was told. Victims, in discovery of what had happened to their beloved lost family members, perpetrators in recognition of the impact that they had had on the lives of both the living and the dead and notably Archbishop Desmond Tutu himself frequently in tears as he presided over the hearings. It forced a nation to refocus on values which had been lost to us in our struggle for freedom from the apartheid regime. Our battle together from all different sides of the debate was being held publicly, in a participative way, allowing for salvation in recognition and washed away by tears. There was a lot more to the TRC in terms of the legal constructs and the work behind the scenes to bring about a sense of fairness and justice but the public face of it did more than can ever be measured simply because we shall never know what catastrophic consequences would have overwhelmed our fledgling democracy, had we not embarked upon that bridge to forgiveness.

In no way do I suggest that we could ever forget the ghastliness of the tragedy suffered by so many through the apartheid years, nor that the deeply held personal pain suffered in the disclosure of truth could ever be whitewashed. It will (and should) remain with us as a reminder of how our treatment of each other should never be repeated but it should also be a golden lesson to us in how we manage the future of our lives and those of our future generations.

So for these reasons, writing the commission reports, identifying the perpetrators insofar as we were able and in allowing for the stories of those brave enough to come and tell their truths, we were in some small way making a contribution. We were hopefully bringing about some peace at least through clarity of what was going on in the ever increasing spiral of violence in the Crossroads and Philippi areas.

There are, of course, a number of ways to tell the truth. The TRC had identified four notions of truth, these being;

- **Factual or forensic truth** - This by definition is, factual and objective truth established through the careful collation of corroborative evidence, clearly not possible for our Cape Town Commission hearings.

- **Personal or narrative truth** - This relies on personal truths, as people themselves experienced it, giving them a voice to speak of their experiences. This is very much founded on the African values of narrative story telling where much of history has been handed down through oral storytelling. In our commission hearings, participants were listened to in their own languages and in so doing, like the TRC, allowed their stories to be validated simply by giving them a voice with which to speak and be heard. Their voices would be recorded in a formal memory so that at the very least, the history would never be lost.

- **Social or dialogue truth** - Again, as separate and distant from factual truth, social truth is the truth of experience, established through interaction, discussion and debate. So, whilst the perspectives of all the people involved in the conflicts of Crossroads and Philippi was mind-bogglingly complex, it was in many cases totally understandable from the perspectives of our participants. Their experiences had driven them to make partial decisions which were in context, real and tangibly realistic alternatives for them at that time. Like the TRC, we had submissions from all organisations, political, policing, non-governmental organisations, and local government and local community forums. By its very nature, having their participation served to complete the web of complexity and allowed for a level of scrutiny to test emerging awareness of the truth insofar as we were able to verify it in a non-scientific way. It was, therefore, socially true. Whilst this would never satisfy the sceptics, it would satisfy the social need for a truthful depiction of the story as experienced by those who had to live it. It would affirm the humanity of our responses to those stories and restore a sense of dignity to those who had had it repeatedly stripped from them.

- **Healing and restorative truth** - Placing facts and what they mean within the context of human relationships. This was central to the TRC and I like to think, central to our process too. If we could not provide forensic truth to the police authorities, which could then be used to extract a formal justice and thereby some sense of compensation, we could at least make sure that it was told. Then there was hope for acknowledgement and through this, in time an opportunity for restorative healing. Affirmation of pain recognises injury and thereby grants dignity. How many times have each of us, in our own lives, asked the rhetorical question of those who we believe have hurt us, "Why can you not simply recognise/accept accountability for what you have done?" because we know we would be able to rest and even possibly forgive if we believed the hurt was acknowledged? It is the dignity in affirmation of our pain that we seek.

> "I am what I am because of who we all are."

These concepts of truth are the purpose of this book. It is my little contribution to keep the wonder of the truth alive and to tell the story of the courage of people in facing their enemies, despite the formidable risks to themselves; simply in pursuit of the truth for whatever salvation it could give them, even if only for a personal and social truth. In South Africa there is a term called "Ubuntu," it means, "I am what I am because of who we all are" and it is an extraordinary statement of generosity and humanism. It is Africa's lesson to the first world and I love the fact that it is in our ancient ancestry that we are taught that we can only find fulfilment through interacting with one another. It is a statement of kinship which spans race and creed and unites us in a common purpose.

"My humanity is caught up and is inextricably bound up in what is yours..."

ARCHBISHOP DESMOND TUTU

Archbishop Desmond Tutu brought this concept to the TRC in his belief through Ubuntu when he explained that "My humanity is caught up and is inextricably bound up in what is yours…"

John Donne's "No man is an island unto himself…" is the western world's definition of Ubuntu.

"No man is an island unto himself..."

JOHN DONNE

We cannot move forward in our lives unless we face the truth. Not to do so only forces us to keep our eyes firmly focused on the past and not the future and it can only sustain the pain, the horror, the deep unhappinesses we may have suffered. In facing the truth, it allows us at least the chance to let go of the past, to leave it behind and to move on with a greater hope of freedom and vindication if not forgiveness, at least a recognition and acknowledgement of its eventuality. Hope pulls us forward, keeps us going, makes us get up again and fight on.

There is always hope in a rainbow.

What separated the Crossroads/Philippi hearings from the TRC hearings was that we were not promising amnesty. Therefore, we were not able to attract the participation of all the perpetrators, although some did come to make their statements. We were therefore unable to perfectly match the victims to perpetrators and could not claim to have fully met the healing and restorative truth benefit so desperately sought after. It was this residual sense that we did not do enough which has stalked me ever since. I do think, though, that we were able to provide at least for the personal and narrative truth and also for the verification of social truth. I know that further studies of the crises have ensued which have gone deeper and more scientifically into the story.

What we did do, was speak up and publish what we had understood that we had found. Whilst we could not provide evidence to the allegations which we made, we could provide enough of a public voice to make the investigation of those allegations unavoidable. We would try to invoke a political and police response to get action and to deliver leadership to these people. So at the back of the report we included an annexure of the date that statements had been made, the classification of the charge, the complainant's identities and the suspect's identities and whether charges had indeed been laid.

It was a report which is an utter indictment of the criminal justice system. Under the last column, only 28 charges had been laid in 94 cases of multiple murder, arson, looting and complaints of intimidation by identified perpetrators. Of these, 9 had not been progressed because there had been no police follow up. Of those 19 that could have gone to court, it was doubtful that there would be much chance of sentence and incarceration, given the history of the public prosecutor's offices and that of the magistrate's courts.

Given that we were led to believe that 50% of the actual crimes were going unreported, these figures are shamefully damning. The commission was also to learn that there was a backlog of the caseload at the Mitchell's Plain magistrate's court and that the postponement of cases further undermined any chance of conviction. Statistically, we were told in hearings that there had not been one single conviction in 54 cases on the court role at the time of the crisis. As we already knew, the ease with which bail was granted allowed perpetrators to simply remove the threat of witnesses from their cases. The already stretched police investigation force was wasting their time in the defence of bail applications instead of catching all the criminals roaming the streets.

A total overhaul of the system was needed. It was my hope in the writing of the report that we would at least get that overhaul.

CHAPTER 12

10 DECEMBER 1998

Chapter 12

10 DECEMBER 1998

Before the full council of the city of Cape Town, with the press in the gallery, the mahogany of the desks gleaming, the Executive Committee seated in the podium seats, the officials behind them in rank order, the presiding Cape Town City Manager, Andrew Boraine, in charge of proceedings…In front of us sat three of the councillors we had named so fully and thoroughly in the report.

11 December 1998

In a Cape Times article, entitled "Crossroads conflict - Warlords Arm for "99 election,"

"Weapons are being stockpiled and 'warlords' are planning a comeback in time for next year's polls in one of South Africa's most famous shacklands – Crossroads. Willem Steenkamp and Chris Bateman report.

The city council moved to address 20 years worth of internecine violence and power struggles in Crossroads and Philippi that have blocked housing and service delivery. The council warned of an arms build-up and simmering conflicts that threaten to disrupt voting in these areas next year.

A hard-hitting report released yesterday by the City of Cape Town details how the tangled political and social fabric of crossroads and Philippi is evolving, pitting anti-development traditionalists – who fear losing their vice-like financial and political grip on these communities – against new-era pro-development democrats.

The city also says it has heard evidence that a "third force" aligned to the former grouping is stockpiling arms in preparation for fresh conflict.

City Manager and local electoral officer Andrew Boraine said yesterday that he was "concerned" about the trend in Crossroads. The council would debate the report at its next meeting in January but he called for "some sort of summit" of all the political parties in the immediate future to commit to a code of conduct promoting political tolerance..."

In addition to the terms of reference, we had also identified a future threat to safety for everyone. At the time, the papers were full of reports of police stations and defence force depots being broken into and the consequent theft of arms. We knew where many of these weapons were being stockpiled and identified the groups responsible, which followed the allegiances we had articulated. We had been certain that the information would be taken seriously and that immediate action would be taken to deflect any further violence. Our recommendations had included the training of councillors to fulfil their mandates fairly, teaching the communities their rights in government, improving law enforcement and getting political parties to accept accountability and enforce discipline within their ranks, so that economic problems in the areas could be addressed holistically.

The Executive committee Chair, Saleem Mowzer said that the council would study the recommendations and findings carefully.

Andrea Weiss, political reporter for the Cape Argus also wrote on the 11th December 1998, that …

> "rumours of stockpiling of weapons in anticipation of the elections and evidence of violent clashes between opposing political groups which have claimed at least ten lives already this year, are cause for concern.
>
> Fears are that the endemic conflict which has plagued the area since the mid 1980s will escalate in the run-up to the election…."

We recommended immediate action. We were told that as council was in its last meeting before the Christmas break, they would debate the report at their next meeting on or around 20th January 1999. All three of the commissioners, Essa Moosa, Mlamli Mfenyana and I were at pains to insist that more urgent action be taken as we knew more violence was inevitable. We could not have put it more plainly. We begged for a meeting of all the players to build a code of conduct by which means they could hold each other to account in a concerted effort to quell the violence and for the alarming stockpiling of weapons to be investigated immediately. We were told that our report was to be given to the National

Crime Prevention Strategy (NCPS) for their further investigation. I could also only hope that Omar Valley's request that it be given to the Multi-Action Delivery Mechanism (MADAM) involving key people in crime prevention on a provincial and national level (driven by the then Minister of Safety and Security, Sydney Mufamadi) ,would be followed through.

From the pit of my stomach I became aware of a rising sense of panic and despair. How could this room full of bureaucrats sit in the sanctity of council chambers and dismiss the report as being of "concern" but not urgent enough to require action before their Christmas break? I was absolutely, utterly convinced - and we had seen enough evidence of the atrocities to ensure our devoted attention to the fact - that the situation was going to escalate and that more people would die. Formal protocols denied furtherance of the debate. We were simply dismissed…and that was that.

There are few times in my life when the anticlimax was so huge. It overwhelmed us all to the point that we were stunned into a silence which would render us incapable of doing anything other than stare vacantly for at least half an hour. We felt flattened by it, overwhelmed by the ineptitude of the people in leadership who we believed would have to do something with this story.

The three commissioners and our secretariat had been working on this for a solid five months. Our lives had been buried in it, reliving the horrors that the victims had endured every day and every night. We had tried to put their stories into context, organised the complexity into bite sized chunks which could be managed in a planned and constructive way by different groups responsible for different elements all of which, acting in concert, gave the hope of some relief from the spiral of violence we were witness to. We had done what had been asked of us.

And we had failed. Not our masters, those who set us to task, but the people who had trusted us as the last port of call in a world of no justice and no recourse.

In a way, what happened next was at least evidence that we had got under somebody's skin and unsettled them enough to want us silent from that point onward.

CHAPTER 13

A LUTA CONTINUA

THE STRUGGLE CONTINUES

Chapter 13

A LUTA CONTINUA

> "There is a time for departure even when there's no certain place to go."
>
> *TENNESSEE WILLIAMS, CAMINO REAL*

The next day, the newspapers at least covered the précised version of the report. I, together with some of my business partners had taken to the local pub for a long lunch as we mulled over the events of the previous few months. It would have been about 4pm, as we were leaving, that my mobile phone rang and I recognised the caller ID on its screen as one of the close associates working with us on the commission. This was a trusted source and one who had impeccable credentials and connections to the parties that were named.

I was apparently on eight different death lists. Apparently, as it was known that I had all the transcripts in evidence and that the report had largely been collated through my office, I was to be a target. Actually, and much, much more sinister, was a direct threat to my children.

I had been on death lists before. Going right back to my days at Trident Steel and tracking all through my career to that point, I had been threatened - as many in my position in the community we worked in would have been. But the threats had always been aimed squarely at me and I was always in the middle of processes that I knew would be resolved. I would never have responded to these threats if they were levelled at me and me alone but this time they were aimed at my family and I had seen what could be done to families. I had lived with the anguish of the mothers who had had their children taken from them, in front of them, and knew I could never survive that myself.

I remember turning to Steve Woods, my partner in The Achievement Network Africa (TANA) who was waiting for the call to end and saying simply to him,

"We have to leave."

"Yes, ok, we were going anyway, cheers I'll see you tomorrow," he would have said something along those lines.

"No, I mean we have to leave. I have to take my family away."

It was a moment of truth for me, one of absolute clarity and one which I knew would remain with me forever. There was no fear, no histrionics, just a cold and clinical assessment of fact. I had not thought it through, I just knew that there were no alternatives and the only thing worrying me at that point was how much time I'd have to make it happen. I didn't even know what it really meant, I had no idea how it would impact our lives, I just knew we had to act quickly and smartly.

In retrospect, I have to thank so many people in my support group who immediately understood what was happening. I was not the first who this had happened to. Officials in leadership roles, particularly in housing issues, had already left with their families for the UK and the

United States so it was not a new trend. It was just a measure, yet again, of a complete distrust in the criminal justice system that could allow such things to be so real in South Africa at that time.

It was the middle of December and everyone was slowing down for the Christmas and New Year break. We knew that if any action was to be taken, it would probably be targeted at my home or alternatively at our two sons who were going to the local school in St. James where we lived.

I had been told that I did not have much time and so our immediate action was to ensure that we got Kate, our PA, out of my home office asking her to work from Steve's office from that point on. It was a Friday so a good time to make a decision like this work. As it turned out, Kate was to report to us that later the following week when she was there collecting things, a group of decidedly shady characters had attempted to gain access to our office. She had called the police in Muizenburg to attend and they had managed to frighten of the group of four men with their sirens. The local police, through Director Mpembe had been informed of our concerns.

Within five hours of that phone call, we moved our family out of the house to friends and made plans to drive to my parent's holiday home on the beautiful Garden Route of the Western Cape. On the Monday morning we notified the school that the children would not be back at school for the remaining two weeks of term which was okay for that time of year, and we left Cape Town. We would at least buy some time with this opportunity and we would need this to come to terms with the events of the past days.

That holiday was one I will remember forever. It was a time of coming to terms with the decision that our lives had taken a turn unthought of before. When all your future plans that you thought were in place and had worked toward are thrown up in the air, when your very identity and who you thought you were going to grow to be, becomes just a dream which looks increasingly as if the pixels are fading, it is quite a challenge to deal with emotionally. Suddenly we were faced with the question of where we should be going.

My mother had resolutely refused to give up her Australian citizenship and had wisely registered the births of all her children in Australia, giving us a choice which I was about to exercise. I also had an Irish passport by descent through my grandfather and there was some discussion of Ireland as an option. At that time Ireland was in a place of great growth and looked economically sound but we were also thinking of the life our children would need to live. We chose Australia as the country which could offer us a climate and lifestyle closest to the one we were losing.

But Dave and the children had no such passports and whilst they would have been able to travel temporarily, this would have been disruptive to their schooling. Dave had both his garage and service station business as well as his building business to think of. How were we to protect the children, move the whole family and try to keep some balance in place for their sense of security?

We decided that I would have to leave South Africa, taking the transcripts and all evidence in my possession at that time, thus removing the threat from whomever it was that was making these threats. Whether they wanted me to shut up on further notifications, particularly with regard to the arms caches, or to get hold of the transcripts to identify witnesses, I will never know but I suspect a bit of both.

We would apply for residence permits for Australia on the basis of repatriation of my Australian citizenship and Dave would have to immediately sell his businesses, our cars, and hopefully our property so that we could fund the transition.

It was important to sell the cars, since they were easily identifiable and we knew they were a safety risk for us. Dave would have to make do with a rust bucket run-around he used as a garage vehicle. He would also attend school with the two boys until he was assured that they were indeed safe at school and he would have to be there at the start and end of every school day. We would make arrangements to alter the pattern of their everyday lives so that they could not be caught in habitual movements. We have friends and family who rallied around us in the months following and to whom we will always be indebted.

I was on a plane to Sydney in the second week of January, armed only with my credit card and a few Australian dollars. I had two suitcases with me, one filled with the commission evidence and the other with as many business clothes as I could pack because I knew I'd have to find work as soon as possible. We were now on a very strict budget and my flight arrived in Sydney at midnight. Dave and I would only be able to communicate by mobile phone from that point on and we had no idea when we'd see each other again.

Another long lost friend, Nell, was good enough to meet me at Sydney airport, having arranged accommodation for me in a very inexpensive hotel in Randwick. As it turned out, it was inexpensive for a reason. It was directly above a very active pub which was alive and kicking until at least four or five every morning but it was close to where Nell lived with her family and I did not want to endanger anyone else at that stage, preferring to be on my own.

But that first night I was absolutely terrified, sitting on the floor with my back pressed up against two suitcases blocking access/egress against the door. I was too terrified to go to the public bathroom, felt utterly alone and lost without my beloved family. It was then that I felt at my lowest, then that I allowed the reality of all that we had lost to come crashing down on me in my own little wave of despair.

But that was the only time, I think, I indulged my self sorrows! I knew that I would have to start another life now and the strength which comes from knowing that others depend on you to make it happen is a marvellous pick-me-up!

My mission at this time was to find a job, find good schools for the two boys and find a roof over our heads…in that order. I had little or no cash at the time, just what I was able to access on my card, and somehow we were going to have to build a new life, very much as we had had to do 10 years earlier, when we had moved to Cape Town, almost to the day!

My wonderful godmother, Eleanor, who lives in Sydney, rescued me from my lofty accommodations after a few days and I began to wander around Sydney, getting to know the suburbs surrounding the main city and finding my way from employment agency to employment agency, completing personality profile testing until I think I had been through the full gamut of poking through my addled brain! I was becoming increasingly aware of just how short we were on the financial viability scale; at that time it was R4 (four South African rands) to the Aussie dollar. I was also not used to selling myself at all. In my previous life, work had literally walked in through the front door and we were in the incredibly lucky position to be able to turn work away that did not excite us. Now I had to focus on starting again, at the bottom of the resource pile, where no one knew me and no one would be able to relate to my position with ease. I also had little to offer. I knew my capabilities but my fall back position into the world of labour law would not have been attractive to anyone in Australia because I had no demonstrated track record with Australian labour legislation. The fact that we had built our Commission for Conciliation, Mediation and Arbitration (CCMA) very much on the model of the Australian Industrial Relations Commission (AIRC), more recently known as the Fair Work Commission, meant nothing to anyone who was not active in that world. They could not have been blamed for not taking my word for it. Then I had had such a breadth of experience, that when I was asked what my capabilities were, I would confidently answer that I could adjust to just about anything. In my world, true, but in theirs, less than credible.

I was about to taste what it felt like to be alone, homeless (just about), without work, and completely unable to do what I had always done so naturally for all of my adult life…to provide for my family and to stand independently and proudly on my own two feet.

On the day that I looked at a small, two bedroomed, crumbling wooden house with the paint peeling off it and an outside dunny in Bondi and was told the asking price of $500,000, I decided that we would probably have to look elsewhere for our future settlement. It did have a view of the sea if you stood on the dunny seat and craned your neck through the open hole at the back but I was not persuaded that it would keep us warm or dry and as we'd have to borrow the lot in a mortgage it would be unlikely that we'd be able to fix it for a while!

I had bought a ticket with 4 stops in Australia, knowing that I would have to look around and my next stop was Brisbane. There, my eldest brother had settled in 1995 after our father had died and he was happy for me to spend some time with him. As it turned out, a very thorough coverage of all of the major agencies and bigger employers was completed within two weeks and it was clear that the market there wasn't looking for my skills sets.

I flew to Perth on my birthday, 26th February and shared this with some friends who I had worked with in South Africa and who had emigrated a few years earlier. They had established their own consulting company and were doing very well but there would be no room for another consultant for a while. I was beginning to get a little worried and whilst I did talk to a few people in Perth, I was sure that business was in a downturn there too. I'll never forget the ferry owner who took me across to Rottnest Island one day. He had asked a few questions and was emphatic in his view that one could not make money in Australia without having money to begin with. "Give that idea up now, mate. You need money to make money here. You'd be best off to get any job you can and start from there!"

Well, he was probably right. My last ticket stop was supposed to be to Adelaide. For some strange reason I had not thought of Melbourne but the night before I was due to leave Perth I called other great friends of mine, from university days, on the off chance that they'd pick up on an old mobile number I had. They did!

Ray and Renay had immigrated to Melbourne six years before. They had lived in Johannesburg for a further 4 years after we had left for Cape Town and whilst we knew that they'd gone to Australia, I did not know they were in Melbourne. Their invitation to visit and stay with them was warm and persuasive. "Flick Adelaide," they said, "you are much more likely to find work here in Melbourne than in Adelaide."

At that point I was glad to have any advice and as I had been away from everyone I was close to for more than two months, their invitation was too hard to resist.

I will always be grateful to these two dear friends who opened up their home in Caulfield to me. I only stayed with them for two weeks, just to find my feet, but they literally put me back together and talked me through the protocols of how the system worked in Melbourne. They gave me advice and guidance which I desperately needed and company at night with their children, after their work days ended.

I moved into a self serviced apartment in South Yarra, which is a wonderfully alive, vibrant part of the outer city but with the marvellous public transport system, very easily central to everywhere I would need to get to.

I started the slog of registering for work at all the employment agencies in town and whilst everyone was interested in my story, it was clear that my unfocussed response to my skill set was not placing me high on the wanted list.

I was also trying to do a lot of things simultaneously. I had fallen in love with Melbourne, with its arts culture and sports culture, which I knew would appeal to Dave. He is a petrol head and as Melbourne hosts the first of the world circuit Grand Prix annually in March, I knew it would go down well with him. Assuming now that I would eventually get work in the city, I felt relatively certain that I could look for schools which I thought were good enough for the boys and then follow through with an address with close enough access.

Auburn primary school for Thomas, who would be coming into year 5 and Xavier College for James, year 7, were the two schools I had settled on fairly quickly. That left me with a view that we would have to find a house within close enough proximity to both.

What was keeping me awake at night was the method of buying a house. In South Africa, you looked at what was on the market in the newspapers, called the estate agent and then made an offer. Following a bilateral negotiation process, you'd hopefully settle on a price, agree on a transfer date and that was that. Here in Australia, I was faced with an asking price, which was probably not the real price and which would only be determined by the highest bidder on an auction date in the far future. Even then, the seller may not sell and there'd be this "passed in" stage where everyone was in limbo until somehow through the grapevine you might find out that the house had gone for as much as $200 or $300,000 more than the asking price. I was totally dumfounded and completely terrified of this process and consequently made it my mission to attend as many auctions as I possibly could in the hopes that one day I might put my newly learned skills to the test! I think I attended over a hundred auctions, always careful to keep my hands away from any nervous twitching action which could get me into trouble.

And trouble meant that I had no money to complete any offer at all. I went off to the banks to find out how to borrow. Dave had by this stage sold both our cars and the princely sum of $28,000 had been sent to me which I had deposited into the Commonwealth Bank. I was living very frugally, the expense of the apartment being the highest cost and it was expensive. I wanted to get into accommodation that could house us all as soon as Dave could get the family across.

In the meantime, he had also suggested that I buy a family car which we would need when he got here and so I was looking at this as well. I found an old Mitsubishi Pajero at a second hand car lot and was so excited about it that I did not haggle on the price. I should have, as it turned out that I was completely ripped off. It was a 1989 model, had done 179,000 kms and was leaking from the sunroof I had fallen for but at least I was mobile again and it was the first big purchase for us as a family on foreign shores. I don't regret it as it gave us a good two year run, that old car, and successfully got us across the French line (in the desert south of Alice Springs) the following year on our trip "up to see Lake Eyre and Uluru to learn about the DreamTime."

It did mean that the budget was severely hindered and my talks with the banks for a home loan were not looking hopeful. I had found a house that I thought we would be happy in. It was in Burke Road in Camberwell, a beautiful old art deco house which had ample room for us all, albeit a tiny garden. By this stage I had been talking to Dave daily by email - I had changed my email address three times to try and keep us as safe as I could. Dave was keeping me in touch with progress on his side and I was able to assist with seeing officers in immigration in Box Hill on my side. He was up-to-date with my house hunting and school searches and was keeping the boys in the loop to ensure that they were excited about the future and looking forward to the change. We were trying to keep them as forward focused as possible as we knew it would be a wrench for them to leave.

My mother had decided to visit from Stanley, in Tasmania, her home since my father's passing. She was sharing my apartment for the two weeks of her visit and it was her assistance to me in saying she would stand surety for a loan which helped me get the first loan with the Commonwealth Bank. How or why they trusted me on the strength of my resume alone, I will never know. Perhaps it was the desperation in my voice, but I am assured that it would be unlikely that I would get a full mortgage today with only a few cents in the bank and no job in sight. I know they talked to my business associates in South Africa and will have checked out my past credit ratings etc. but again, I shall be forever grateful to them for their trust.

I was beginning to feel a little more confident day by day, as others began to believe in me.

On the Thursday morning, with the confirmation of a loan available to me and a meeting that evening, whereby I was going to formally put in an offer on the Camberwell house in the hopes of getting it off the market prior to the dreaded auction on Saturday, my mother and I took off for a day of relaxation to this mythical place called the Yarra Valley.

Anyone who knows me and my family knows that it takes roughly four hours for my mother and I to rub each other up the wrong way and we inevitably have a volatile outcome, from which we have to return to remake an uneasy friendship. It has been like this all of my life.

On this drive out to the Yarra Valley, for a lunch and coffee, I was driving her little Daihatsu Charade. The first rub was that the "darling little tyres were being caught in the tramline grooves, doing the poor little car enormous and savage damage." I tied to get out of the grooves, gritted my teeth and continued along the way. "You drive too fast. I have never understood why you have to drive so dangerously." "I am trying to kill myself," I replied. "Well you might do that on your own and in your own car," was her response…and so it continued. On the way, I had to stop off at Box Hill for yet another stressful encounter regarding immigration matters for the children and so was more than a little stressed by the time we reached Lilydale. Although this was definitely not the Yarra Valley it was as far as I was taking mother. We got out of the car and my mother, not unlike myself, unfortunately decided to make me go to precisely the last place I wanted to enter…the local estate agent. She marched in despite all my protestations about time wasted as we had our house buying meeting that evening!

Well, sometimes, if you can't beat 'em…so I marched in behind her and demanded to see "that house in the window." The somewhat startled agent began spluttering that "this is the country and we need to make appointments to see houses on the market especially when they are open for inspection pending auctions etc." to which I responded (whilst expelling all the air I had been holding in my lungs; very relieved) "that is a pity since we only have today" and to which my mother loudly reacted, "oh don't be ridiculous Geraldine, of course we don't need to see any properties, you win this round" and we both marched out again in search of that elusive coffee.

We had managed about a hundred yards when the estate agent came trotting up behind us to say that he had "secured a viewing, due to limited time etc. etc. and would we please follow him, as it was some way out in the country but he'd be happy to drive." Rarely have I seethed so much; sitting in the back of that car, the agent chatting merrily to my mother in the front seat as we drove through Lilydale and out into the country. I tried to make sense of this. How absolutely bizarre. As if I did not have enough on my plate to worry about. I had the schools sorted, the house I would hopefully secure that evening and then after that I would surely find a job in the city which was miles and miles away from this place that I now found myself in. I made up my mind to continue with the gritted teeth and throbbing temple position and just endure, breathing steadily so as not to risk an explosion. I would simply keep my own counsel until I could get back on the road to Melbourne that evening.

We arrived at this property, having turned off a main road onto dirt and I smugly ticked another "wrong!" box off in my head as we rattled our way up hill and down dale. We had to park outside and walk into the garden. We could not see the house as the lady who lived there had recently had a hip operation and was bedridden. I was anxious to reassure the agent that we did not want to disturb her and that seeing the house really was not necessary "as my husband can fix anything, being a builder."

We began the walk into the driveway and immediately I was aware of an incredibly strong sense of well-being. It was unlike anything I have ever experienced before. I felt it hit me in the centre of my chest. It felt like home. It was overpowering and left me feeling quite knocked out. I could not explain it. It was the furthermost thought in my mind and I was already fighting any sense of breaking my resolve of not one minute before. The trees were in Autumnal regalia. The colours were spectacular, oranges, bronzes, coppers, engine reds, yellows, ambers and all the different shades of green. Whoever had planted this garden had known what they were doing with it. It was beautifully natural, full of gorgeous shrubs, camellias and rhododendrons, azaleas and hibiscus and all of the deciduous trees, planted strategically in total harmony with huge majestic native gums, guarding aspects of the garden like sentries. Their different bark structures were already a study in fascination for me.

We walked anti-clockwise around the five acre property. I remember every step as at last we crested the hill from one side of the land to the other and we were immediately overawed by the most beautiful view across the Warburton ranges and behind them, the majestic Dandenong ranges.

By this time, my mother and I were in furious agreement that this was indeed a very beautiful property and we loved everything about it despite it being in the middle of nowhere, or so it felt at the time. We were chatting away to this agent who was by all later accounts highly amused at these weird women who had appeared out of nowhere. We wandered around the garden again, still not having seen the house at all, which we could see was a regular brick built home of no particular attraction, but all I was aware of was this constant buzzing in my head, "This feels like home, what am I going to do…I feel that this is where I am supposed to be, what on earth is going on in my head and how am I going to manage the next step?"

CHAPTER 14

HOME AGAIN

Chapter 14

HOME AGAIN

I told my mother that I was going to phone the agent for the Camberwell house and tell them that we would not be coming in at 5pm that evening as we had been delayed. She was a little concerned at this but accepted it as she was enjoying herself being entertained by this other agent who was later to take us on a little drive through the beautiful Yarra Valley and to see some other properties in his portfolio. All the while, my mind was in a quandary.

Later that night I sent an urgent email to Dave, explaining that suddenly there was this new opportunity and giving him a chance to talk to the boys about it. He came back almost immediately. He was in no way unclear.

“Buy the Camberwell property. You have been on about this for a month. You have done all the work which makes this a sensible decision. I don’t want to live in the middle of nowhere. James agrees. Thomas, on the other hand, says that if he can have a horse, buy the farm. Joke.”

“How much do you think the sellers will accept for that property we saw today?” I asked the agent on the phone. He gave me a price and it was exactly the same as the amount confirmed by the bank that day as a potential loan.

“I’d like to put in an offer to them please but can you make it conditional that they will let us settle at least by the end of June?” Dave had also confirmed that day that the papers for himself and the children had come through as a result of our morning visit to immigration in Box

Hill. It was the 15th of April, 1999. By midnight that day, I had bought our new home.

It was not the home that any of us had thought of before but what was I to do in the face of such an overwhelming sense of a decision being so right? To this day, I am absolutely convinced that my father and brother Andrew were directing traffic from on high because we were later to discover that the Camberwell house went on to auction and earned a full $200,000 more than I would ever have been able to afford. I am sure that they were looking after us all and that had it gone any other way, there would have been yet another disaster to face. Breaking the news to my mother who had retired the night before while all arrangements were being made was another challenge but, as the years have moved on, she has been known to take all the credit for a very good idea at the time!

Dave was quite another matter and I really do understand the stunned silence (to which I was rightfully subjected over the next two days) during which time he must have battled to come to terms with these new events. He tells me that he really did worry about what on earth we'd do in the bundu, (middle of nowhere) - previously described from initial thoughts myself.

With a cheery "au revoir" to my mother who was returning to Tasmania, I moved from the South Yarra apartment to the Lilydale Motel as the new focus of schools and the transition to finding work now as a commuter of some considerable distance dawned upon me. My accommodation was a LOT less attractive to me as there was little or no street life in Lilydale and I had to transfer my morning trot around the Tan (Melbourne's famous running track of 11 kilometres around the gorgeous botanical gardens), for a morning triple trot around Lilydale Lake. It was a lonely time for me and the only time I could remember since my 24th birthday, that I weighed a good 30kgs less than I do now.

But I had things to do, especially getting the boys registered in school. Whilst we changed Thomas within the first term of his arrival from the local Seville Primary to St. Mary's in Mt. Evelyn, getting James into Mt. Lilydale Mercy College was a good call and all three of the children have been through their good portals.

I began a very serious search for work. If settlement was to take place on the 29th of June, 1999, the day our family would finally settle permanently in Australia, I would have to pay at least an interest payment by the 29th of July that year. With no job in sight and funds running dangerously low, I was worried.

> "The most important kind of freedom is to be what you really are. You trade in your reality for a role. You trade in your sense for an act. You give up your ability to feel and in exchange, put on a mask. There can't be any large-scale revolution until there's a personal revolution, on an individual level. It's got to happen inside first."
>
> *JIM MORRISON*

One of the employment agents I had been to see before called me into town. Geoff Hopkins, then working for Tanner Menzies as a senior search consultant, had asked me, "What is it that you want to do, what is it that you are good at?" I had given him my "anything and everything" response, given that I was really prepared to do absolutely anything to get back into the job market. He had studied me quietly and then he told me to remain silent while I listened to him.

He launched into one of the strongest lectures that I have ever endured, telling me that I needed to refocus myself with greater clarity. Telling me that I had to absolutely stop feeling sorry for myself, that no-one was interested in my story in Australia. What they were interested in was what I had to offer. That I was capable of adding value to their business, that I was eager to get involved in a new life focused on their success etc." I listened and remember clearly feeling misunderstood, my blood beginning to boil as he came to the end of a very long soliloquy. On cue, with the indication that he had finished, I launched back at him with a deliberate and clipped clarity enunciating my skills capability in short, sharp sentences.

"Now that's what I was looking for," he said and we settled into a discussion about potential opportunities. I have thanked Geoff at every opportunity when I have bumped into him over the past fourteen years and will continue to do so. He taught me a lesson never to be forgotten. He awoke in me a realisation that if I was going to make it happen in Australia, I'd have to focus forwards and it is a lesson I keep reliving as life continues to happen at an ever increasing pace. Nose pointed firmly into the future, the core strength in resilience and survival.

I was not to find a job until the beginning of August, five weeks into having safely landed my beloved family in Australia. Despite the despair, the worry, the absolute terror in thinking I had caused the biggest mistake in my life and that of my husband and three children, I wore a face which at least bore the visage of confidence and assurance. I would dress professionally every morning and travel into town by train, looking at people who had jobs, knowing that hollow feeling inside of a responsibility and utter helplessness without work which we had to have to complete a transition from one world to the next.

On the day I was offered a job, I remember standing on a street corner in the city, praying for help.

CHAPTER 15

Settlers

Chapter 15

SETTLERS

"Go where you have never been before. Dream up a destination, a path to follow, a wildest unknown way, over rocks and scrag, across high hills where the wind bites cold with malice, through deep mysterious valleys where the wild things roar and echo and rumble and stamp and hiss great clouds of steam from their terrible huffing ways.

Dream the impossible dream and start walking towards it.

On the way you'll be beaten up, chewed, spat out, mauled, ripped apart, given up for lost. Quite soon you'll learn what it feels like to be beaten up, chewed, spat out, mauled, ripped apart, and given up for lost.

This is called experience and it's very, very valuable in life because what you mostly learn from it is that you were more afraid of what might happen than what did happen. Most successful outcomes are achieved by calling a series of conventional bluffs.

One bright sunny morning you'll discover that the wild and unknown way you took is carpeted with moss and strewn with tiny flowers. It has become a familiar path, a well trodden direction which has put you miles ahead of anyone else and much, much closer to achieving your once impossible dream.

Take the Hero's Journey; find your spirit and live your dreams."

BRYCE COURTENAY

Two weeks into my first role in Australia, I was shattered to get a call from Dave to say that one of our beloved dogs, our German Shepherd, Muppett, who he had put into quarantine in South Africa three months prior to that, had died just prior to being flown to Australia. That loss, that last blow, sent me careening down a steep slope in what felt like an unstoppable break. Luckily, as I had to catch a train to get home, I was forced to put my face back together otherwise I think I might have let it all go that day. We were all devastated as our dogs were to be our last remaining stamp on our resettlement. Not only were they significant members of our family but they signalled the completion of our shift. Dave had told me that when he had said goodbye to them in April in Cape Town, he had felt so terribly sad that he himself had broken down, not sure that he would ever see them again. Dave is not an emotional man, known for his stoic strength, keeping his thoughts shielded from public scrutiny with his easy acceptance of most things. It would have cost him enormously just to tell me this, let alone acknowledge publicly his feelings for our dogs. When I got home, it was to a very sad little family, all of whom needed to be loved.

Which brings me to that bright and sunny realisation in hindsight, when you recognise that mossy, flower strewn path. A sigh of relief when we realised that we were all together and we were all stronger for the experience.

Fundamentally, I would have to admit that the person who had the most to learn through all of this, was me. In my previous life, whilst I was working hard and being successful, I was not there for my family. It was largely Dave who had to hold us all together; Dave, who although he had two businesses to run, was more present for our children than I was. In walking through this fire of change, I had fallen from a highly recognised place in my world of work, to a place where no one knew me at all. The playing field had been completely levelled and I found myself floundering, unable to find an anchor or anything that would enable me to find secure footing on the ground.

In the end, my amazingly patient husband and my wonderful children saved me, none of whom ever judged me or my wild and strange decisions which resulted in the complete uprooting of their own worlds.

In order to enable me to continue working, we had agreed that Dave would be a "stay-at-home-dad" while the children settled. Rachel was only two and half, James twelve and a half and Thomas, eleven.

Our home in Seville became our haven. The boys could ride their bicycles with free abandon where previously they had only been allowed to ride infrequently and always with adult supervision. They would disappear for hours every day, allowing Dave to ponder how he and Rachel would spend their time together.

In the very first few weeks of our arrival we had had no furniture and were living on the tightest budget for food, fuel, etc. and there was little left over for entertainment. Dave had managed once again to secure his last 144 bottles of the very best in his wine collection and without any alternative, we had enjoyed drinking exceptional wines in the evenings while he was contemplating all this extra time he had at home. Two plus two equals one very good little acre and a half under vines, which now, 14 years down the line, provide us with our annual needs plus a boutique label for Red Tin Shed wines, which we sell locally.

Our boys have both grown and begun their own careers now and Rachel is in the final years of her schooling. Who knows what next but this home, which is the one we have lived in longest, has been the saving of us all. As I write the final chapters of this book, I am bathed in sunlight in my office, overlooking that magnificent view, filled with that inner peace that comes from knowing that all that roaring, rushing, terrifying water is well under the bridge now. Our two darling family dogs lie at my feet and my chickens roam freely in a beautiful garden.

CHAPTER 16

LEARNINGS OF LEADERSHIP

Chapter 16

LEARNINGS OF LEADERSHIP

"When I despair, I remember that all through history the way of Truth and Love have always won. There have been tyrants and murderers, and for a time, they can seem invincible, but in the end, they always fall. Think of it - always."

MAHATMA GANDHI

I have talked a lot about my personal learnings of these events, and so won't belabour these. But there are many issues which, on reflection are great insights for those who want to help our developing worlds, and I think they are basic truths. They relate to the myths that bind us to decisions which can have lasting and sometimes devastating effects on the people they are intended to help.

Firstly, poverty is a terrible driver. It makes animals of mankind. Some of us become submissive and completely incapable of resistance against those that it turns into bullies and murderers. It eats away at self confidence and has us unable to find any salvageable self esteem. It leaves us feeling worthless in some cases, and beyond redemption in other cases. Herein lies the ability or permission to be reduced to a savagery which is so incomprehensible to those who have no reference point in feeling it. It means that assumptions of what is normal in the ruling of society as we know it miss the mark by miles. Every time.

So, assuming that one's worldview can be taken as universal when planning development for poor nations, is to treat planning itself as superficial. We must first understand that diversity in itself generates a different way of thinking. We need to understand those differences and to build ideas, from the ground upwards, with the very people who will have to live with those ideas. Generation of ideas is always more creative and richer for the breadth of the engagement. Clearly, in our Crossroads world, the complete failure to engage all parts of a community by council officials and their elected political representatives, led to a total failure in the delivery of any development.

The assumption that the poor and destitute living in shanty self built homes, would want to move into bricks and mortar permanent homes, where they would have to be subject to legal and financial obligations of formal home ownership (rates and service charges) has proved radically wrong. Our world view of what we should all want by way of our living standards is justifiably based on sustainable urbanisation, but when you are talking to people who have never had right of tenure, who have moved at will from place to place in a state of permanent impermanence, it is just one way of thinking this through.

It became increasingly apparent to us working in the commission that there were social issues like safety, security, a sense of community which needed to be addressed before the material issues could be agreed upon. The Women of the WPG had understood this and attempted to take a strong stand, establishing their own legitimate identity and demanding engagement. They had legitimate complaints and sought initially to gain the attention of the authorities by staging a sit-in. They got caught up in a spiral of retaliatory violence, when they believed they were themselves under attack, and seemed to have lost their way at some point. But the responsibility for the origination of conflict must surely rest with a lack of leadership from council and its representatives, who gave no guidance, and no support to direct engagement of the whole community, leading as it should have in an objective, impartial and caring way.

Secondly, the ethics of the councillors were clearly driven by personal interests. Whilst direct corruption was not proved in the hearings, there was more than ample suspicion and that means that a fundamental requirement of good leadership and trust, simply was not there. These councillors had not risen above themselves for the greater good, they were firmly ensconced in their own personal and more immediate needs.

Transparency, brought about through an open debate of the issues would presumably have raised all of the issues onto the table. Individual interests could have been dealt with so as to take them off the table, instead of allowing them to fester and develop into violent outcomes with the most terrible of consequences for everyone involved.

Clearly, partisan relationships and allegiances stemmed from deep rooted traditional rationalities from whence the warlords got their power. The warlords who taxed residents of informal settlements for their right to occupation, clearly pitched them up against any attempts to formalise occupation rights. Yet these same warlords were members of the ruling National Party at that time in the Western Cape, on the Provincial level. These are allegiances which should have been exposed on an open platform, not for anything other than the purpose of transparency, so that everyone had the opportunity to be clearly informed of the drivers for personal interests. If you can see the threat, it's always so much easier to manage it.

To leave it in obscure places allows criminality to breed. The opportunistic nature with which criminal parties became involved in the conflict is in itself founded in relationships or networks of support through affiliations to belief systems. So Ngxobongwana and Nongwe's relationship to PAGAD and their 'Qibla' youth, the councillors to the taxi mafia of the 'Big Eight' gang.

Politics should never be separated from socio-economic and cultural issues. To ignore everyday life, is to pretend that it does not exist and that in itself leads to no trust. It effectively undermines credible leadership.

It is the same in the boardroom. A leader placed into a position of power, not because he/she has any legitimate skill or leadership authority, who runs to the agenda of others in control, ignoring the realities of the organisational trend, culture and living issues, is quickly spotted and disrespected. Continued denial of that truth in itself, leads to a rot of misbehaviour which sets in, just as the level of dishonesty within the organisation breeds permission through lack of leadership to see it cauterised. It is the response of cowards, not leaders, and it leaves those who trust in the legitimacy of leadership sorely short changed.

I have seen this happen myself. It is the saddest thing. When an organisation filled with people of talent and potential, are forced to work for a puppet who lacks the courage to challenge the puppet masters, often driven by a political agenda and consumed by personal interests themselves, the talent leaves or becomes assimilated in bad behaviour.

And so it is that I have always reflected on the greatness of a true leader of influence in my life - Nelson Mandela. who as I write lies ailing in his bed. He will leave a legacy of iconic leadership behaviour which is respected throughout the world. What a truly deserving hero this man is. He was born to lead.

His birth name is Rolihlahla Mandela. Given to him by his father, it is a Xhosa name meaning, "pulling the branch of a tree". It is such a wonderfully appropriate name for him. He yanked the chain of the most powerful oppressors of his country and suffered their wrath. But in doing so, he caught the attention of the world and from prison rose to lead that country with the unbelievably strong message of salvation;

> "To be free is not merely to cast off one's chains, but to live in a way that respects and enhances the freedom of others."
>
> *QUOTED FROM HIS BOOK, LONG WALK TO FREEDOM.*

He is a man who recognised his own human frailties and was not afraid of exposing these to others.

> "Never forget that a saint is a sinner who keeps on trying."
>
> *NELSON MANDELA*

"Never forget that a saint is a sinner who keeps on trying", he wrote to his wife Winnie Mandela from Kroonstad Prison in 1975, and on recognising his past history as a bit of a chauvinist;

> "Sitting down in jail and reading, you discover things which you have never known, and that is one advantage of being in prison, to read literature that opens your mind and makes you realise that some of your ideas in the past were completely wrong."
>
> *NELSON MANDELA*

"Sitting down in jail and reading, you discover things which you have never known, and that is one advantage of being in prison, to read literature that opens your mind and makes you realise that some of your ideas in the past were completely wrong."

In a few, short grabs of his thoughts, lie nuggets of leadership;

- Self reflection, recognition of frailty, learning and modification of behavior to strive to do better;

- The imperative to engage and embrace others' rights to their freedoms and the liberty to live and act in a mutuality of respect.

- The courage to be completely unafraid that there may be others who can do things better than you can, and the generosity of spirit to let them do it.

- The strength to stand up for your beliefs, no matter the risk to yourself, because it is the right thing to do.

- The optimism and resilience to look for and find the advantage in every situation, no matter how dire the circumstances.
- That true leaders are humble and to lead from there.

I have learned through his example, the privilege of leadership as opposed to the imposition of leadership through authority. It is this that gives such dignity to the man who so many revere.

I have learned that through adversity, if you have an open mind, there is hope to be found and that whenever we feel despair, to dig deeply into oneself to find that strength to walk toward it, head held high.

It is, like Gandhi says, "the way of Truth and Love will always win". But Madiba, has shown us, that you have to be Brave too.

There is a real fear that when he goes, there will not be the same level of leadership to continue with his mission, to get things to be "better in the long run". But all of us in this world would be doing him a great disservice if we let him down. If we could all adopt these basic, simple truths of leadership, the world would be a better place.

There's still a way to go. In one of his most famous quotes;

"I have walked that long road to freedom. I have tried not to falter; I have made missteps along the way. But I have discovered the secret that after climbing a great hill, one only finds that there are many more hills to climb. I have taken a moment here to rest, to steal a view of the glorious vista that surrounds me, to look back on the distance I have come. But I can only rest for a moment, for with freedom, come responsibilities, and I dare not linger, for my long walk is not ended."

Indeed, it is not, but it seems that others must now pick up the mantle and share that load. Go in honour and peace and love, Madiba.

The people who came to the Commission to tell their stories, came to have the truth be told, insofar as that truth would in some small way release the horror of what had happened to them. They did so with courage, despite the fear, with the hope that they would regain some of their dignity simply in the telling of their stories, to reclaim something of themselves from the ashes of their homes and their lost lives. In so doing, they earned my respect, and I sincerely hope in the lessons they taught me, there is some learning for others.

Be brave and be truthful to yourself always.

A FINAL WORD FROM THE AUTHOR

In writing this book, I wanted to do two things:

1. Open up some of the truth around a history which, in an uncompromising way, changed my life. But I wanted mostly to concentrate on what I had been told by people whose own lives had been turned upside down. While I can't identify them for fear that I may still bring about some dreadful consequence to them, it is a story which in its own truth, should be told for them.

2. Look at what we can learn about leadership and some of the universal lessons in development planning for organisations with a mission to do good deeds for those in poverty stricken and disenfranchised communities.

What makes these characters stand out in the leadership debate? They were all leaders, some would remain so, some would retreat only to reappear later on the field and some would grow in strength, power and influence to continue in what is a highly contributory way to their communities. Their styles, character, knowledge and skills, their value systems and ethical standards all differed.

Thabethe Simon Mpembe impressed the commission with his intimate knowledge of the area he had inherited half way through 1998.

When he joined the South African police force in 1978 as a rookie he had a big vision which he talks about constantly and consistently, to "transform the police force into a respected, trusted enforcer of the law, to be respected and reinforced by the new constitution of South Africa."

At the time, given the appalling circumstances in which the police force found itself, it would have been one of the biggest, most insurmountable mountains to climb. To join the police force under the apartheid regime, you would either have had to have been desperate, or incredibly naïve, or with criminal intent, knowing that you could abuse the powers of the "law" to your own benefit; desperate, because the police force was notoriously badly paid. If you needed to supplement your income, it was well known that many in the police force, of all racial groups had succumbed to temptation and corruption. They could be "bought" for a price and so it was that many arrested prisoners "escaped" before charges were laid; those who were charged, were often not charged with the serious crimes they had committed but for spurious ones which required no incarceration; those who should have been imprisoned, often received bail sentences (and were bailed by their criminal mates) and those who were imprisoned often "escaped" prison or were granted parole very quickly. The leniency went right the way through to the magistrates courts and the public prosecutor's offices. It took Mandela to insist that serious crimes, rape, arson and murder, were to result in non-bail sentences. This was in 1998, right at the time commissioner Mpembe took office as the Commissioner of Police based in Nyanga.

He had the courage to go after the criminals and then he had the courage to sift through his own police force to catch the corrupt cops and clean them out. The rest of the criminal justice system took note and it was this Director who was credited for his assistance in dealing with PAGAD, which by 2000 had largely been squashed.

So he demonstrated two key leadership principles and lived them every day - a great vision and a courageous preparedness to face down his enemies and take action. Every day, he walked tall with this very strong sense of purpose and steered his own pathway through a cesspool of iniquitous reality, pain and heartache. This resilient leadership earned him respect for the work he was doing and, I think, saved him from the many bullets which I am sure were aimed directly at him as we progressed through the hearings. He lived in the community and it would have been quite easy, I imagine, to get to him. He would have had to be vigilant in every encounter he had.

It would have been a lonely task because when you are at the front of a crisis of this size and gravity, there would be few courageous enough to stand with you. To be brave is one thing, to be prepared to be lonely and brave is the mark of a true leader.

He was not brazen about it. Instead, he demonstrated great empathy and compassion in his understanding of the issues.

He was a thinker, having graduated with a National Diploma in Police Administration, a B Tech Degree and a Masters in Public Administration. He had clearly grasped the importance of listening (and hearing) the needs, concerns and hope of the people in his community and he seemed to respond with humility and total integrity. At the time of writing, Simon Mpembe is the Limpopo Provincial Commissioner, having been appointed from Nyanga to Operational Commander in Cape Town, to Major General in Gauteng, responsible for the for the province's support services, to Area Commissioner of the Vaalrand, based in the Johannesburg Central Police Station (formerly the hated John Vorster Square). It has been a stellar career, achieved quietly, resolutely and with dignity and integrity. A job well done so far.

Our commission findings on Mpembe are transcribed as follows;

"The police personnel are highly de-motivated and demoralised and therefore, would be susceptible to bribery and corruption opportunities. This needs to be taken up as a matter of urgency at

> both provincial and national government levels in order to ensure the arrest of suspects and successful prosecution of suspects. Director Mpembe's attempts at investigation are to be highly commended. His attempts at negotiation with conflicting parties within the communities merit commendation. His attempts to consult with civic bodies and other political organisations requires commendation. His recommendations towards the creation and delivery of recreational facilities need to be given due consideration."

Indeed, in testimony to the leadership of the man, Mpembe was seconded early in 1999 to Operation Good Hope and did not return to his duties at Nyanga police station until the second half of 2000. At the end of this year, he was promoted to the Assistant Provincial Commissioner's role in Gauteng. He had not had the time to develop a strong team behind him and sadly, policing in Nyanga regressed to reactive response, incompetent and negligent investigation and reporting and total mistrust between different constituencies.

I have no idea what happened to the councillors and the warlords, whether they grew to lead, or fell over and never recovered.

What I do know is that in the months after the commission delivered its report and findings, the violence did escalate as we had predicted, arms continued to be taken from police stations and newspapers continued to report on the violence. It was a great pity that more notice was not taken of our warnings at the time and action taken to avert more harm.

For myself, I have always tried to raise my children with this philosophy - The definition of integrity is the courage to say the things you need to say, even at the expense of yourself sometimes. You cannot afford to waste your life by drifting through it allowing others to drive your bus. Your reward is that you can sleep at night (albeit often alone) in the knowledge that you have told the truth - at least to yourself. You may not always be right - in fact, the plight of the brave is often to be wrong! And then to recognise this with candour. The truth stands proud, unprepared to bargain for anything less than the recognition of courage and honesty of conviction. The only rider to this is to do all this with compassion, with the lessons of Madiba, in mutuality of respect.

The writing of this book has signalled yet another transformation in my life. I stepped out of my corporate life a little disillusioned but in working through this book, I feel myself becoming more visible again, less afraid and more certain that I will find my feet again on a different platform and one where I can make a meaningful difference in the community. Once again, the crucible of life will generate more energy to evolve again into another hopeful future. I think I have been circling this project for years – in ever smaller circumferences but still around and around until I have arrived at the point of no return. Thank you for reading it.

> "We have, at last, achieved our political emancipation. We pledge ourselves to liberate all our people from the continuing bondage of poverty, deprivation, suffering, gender and other discriminations. Never, never and never again shall this beautiful land experience the oppression of one by another.... The sun shall never set on so glorious a human achievement. Let freedom reign. God bless Africa.
>
> *NELSON MANDELA, shortly after his inauguration as State President of South Africa, 1994.*

We must continue to fight for this great vision.

CAPE ARGUS, FRIDAY, DECEMBER 11, 1998

Crossroads conflict rooted in past

Old warlords, new democrats battle for control

The deadly political harvest being reaped today in Crossroads has its roots in a deep-seated conflict between the patronage of the old warlords and the new order of elected council representatives.

POLITICAL REPORTER

Ten people have died and more than 40 homes have been razed this year as a result of simmering political conflict.

A three-month sit-in by the Crossroads Women's Power Group this year is what sparked an independent inquiry commissioned by the City of Cape Town, but the roots of the current conflict reach back to the 1970s.

The commission, chaired by acting judge Essa Moosa, outlines a long history of conflict in which those with power could reap the most financial rewards from people desperate for housing and security of tenure.

The report notes: "This pattern of conflict repeats itself from 1986 to the present time. It is based on the control of people, the allocation of sites and the financial returns to those in control. Government concessions granted to those who assumed leadership positions within informal settlement areas created a conflict of interests for those who must have much to lose with the present objectives of structured housing, where rates, taxes and rent are payable to the local authority, and not to community leaders."

The commission drew from the earlier Goldstone Commission Report, set up by former president F W de Klerk, for some of its analysis.

The Goldstone findings were that many people settled in Crossroads as a result of increased urbanisation in the Western Cape after the independence of the Transkei in the mid-1970s.

Immigrants deemed to have broken influx control laws were frequently harassed and their shacks demolished. Then former minister of co-operation and development Piet Koornhof concluded an agreement with the Crossroads Committee, dominated by Johnson Ngxobongwana, that people living at Crossroads would be enumerated and granted temporary rights.

The effect of the Koornhof Agreement was to make Crossroads a desirable place to live for those in the region "illegally", and this special dispensation resulted in a rapid rise in the population of the area.

At this stage, Mr Ngxobongwana, who was in charge of three out of four sections in the area, realised he had something to sell and began charging people to have their names on the list.

Later the government decided that people should "voluntarily" relocate to Khayelitsha after only phase one of the redevelopment of Crossroads had taken place. Those who gained access to the new Crossroads development were predominantly members of Mr Ngxobongwana's group, while another leader in the area, a Mr Memani, moved his people to KTC. Others moved to Khayelitsha under the leadership of Mali Hosa.

The inquiry noted that it was widely believed that, during a term in Pollsmoor Prison in the mid-1980s, Mr Ngxobongwana, formerly considered a progressive activist, was "turned" by the then government.

"What followed in 1986 was a well-documented war between the state-supported 'witdoeke' and the anti-apartheid 'comrades'."

In 1988, Mr Ngxobongwana was elected mayor of Crossroads, retaining an informal system of headmen. But the election tension between Mr Ngxobongwana and his rival, Jeffrey Nongwe, one of his former headmen, led to open warfare leaving many people dead and wounded.

Eventually Mr Ngxobongwana moved to Driftsands near Khayelitsha with about 2 000 followers, and Mr Nongwe assumed the leadership in 1990, being the chairman of the local ANC branch.

Depoutch Elese, an MK-trained activist, returned to the Western Cape where he set up an ANC branch in the Unathi section.

Agreement: former minister Piet Koornhof

List to sell: Johnson Ngxobongwana

Rival: Jeffrey Nongwe

The report says that in 1992, the youth began rejecting the "traditional and patriarchal style of leadership, such as allegedly exhibited by Mr Nongwe, turning more towards the democratised activism allegedly espoused by Mr Elese through the SACP/ANC alliance".

In the 1991/92 taxi war, members of the "Big Eight" gang allegedly connected to Mr Nongwe were involved in the killing of three people at Mr Elese's house.

While violence continued to simmer in the area, no new development took place until after the local elections in 1996, when Mr Elese won the election for ward 18 in the area.

The Crossroads Women's Power Group, which staged the sit-in in January this year, was found to have links with Mr Ngxobongwana and Mr Nongwe, as well as parties disenchanted by and alienated from the ANC, such as the Pan Africanist Congress, the National Party and the United Democratic Movement.

The latest conflict resulted from conflict between two groupings that could "loosely be termed pro-development and anti-development".

"Although beneath the outward disagreement on the progress of housing development in the area, seems to lie political aspirations and old rivalries, in fact virtually the full spectrum of political parties seem to now be involved in the conflict."

The build-up of tension in Crossroads began in January, when the women's group rose to prominence and occupied the municipal offices, ostensibly in protest against the size of houses being built.

Another issue in the area was that the nearest police station was without a commissioner and lacked leadership. The police thus kept out of the rising tension for fear of being accused of partisanship.

The pattern of conflict in Crossroads was founded on battles for territory and power. While some of the grievances of the women's group were genuine, others were not.

"Overwhelmingly, given the history of Crossroads, the primary cause of violence in the Crossroads area would seem to have been, and is, a fight for power and dominance based on territorial leadership driven by personal needs for financial income and power," the report noted.

"On another level, this same fight could be viewed as one between the political 'winners', that being those who gained leadership through the democratic elections process of 1996, and the political 'losers', those who did not gain support during the election, but who had stood for election based on their previous leadership roles in the community."

Councillors, however, did not come away from the inquiry lightly. They, too, were jointly and severally accused of being involved in attacks against members of the community, and also of not taking community grievances seriously enough.

Councillors were also accused of deliberately obstructing meetings of people they perceived to be political opponents.

Councillors for the area should have been more vigilant and circumspect in what they did and said.

Among the report's chief recommendations is that all political parties ensure they have a code of conduct, and that they teach members the basic rules of democracy.

"The primary cause of violence was found by the commission to be party rivalry between political parties, civic bodies, their leaders and members. The commission feels strongly that the organisations should take political responsibility for the conduct and actions of their members," the report concluded.

Danger alert on Crossroads polls

ANDREA WEISS
POLITICAL REPORTER

A clear warning has been sounded that unless a culture of political tolerance takes root in violence-plagued Crossroads and Philippi, there can be no free or fair elections there next year.

Rumours of stockpiling of weapons in anticipation of the elections and evidence of violent clashes between opposing political groups, which have claimed at least 10 lives already this year, are cause for concern.

Fears are that the endemic conflict which has plagued the area since the mid-1980s will escalate in the run-up to the election.

This is one of the main findings of a 300-page report documenting the background to a three-month sit-in by members of the Women's Power Group at the Ikapa municipal offices earlierthis year.

The independent commission of inquiry, chaired by acting judge Essa Moosa, was set up by the City of Cape Town to investigate allegations against councillors and city officials working in the area, primarily around issues of housing and services.

Mr Moosa was assisted by the Rev Mlamli Mfenyana, a respected religious leader in the area, and Geraldine Coy, who serves on the panel of the Independent Mediation Service of South Africa.

The report, released to the full council yesterday, notes that on July 31 this year, police records reflected 82 cases related to the 1998 political violence in Old Crossroads, including 10 cases of murder, 21 cases of attempted murder and 40 cases of arson.

The three commissioners found that the primary cause of conflict in Crossroads and Philippi related to political intolerance between parties, organisations and individuals. These differences were exploited by criminal elements.

City manager Andrew Boraine said there was an urgent need for a summit of political parties to inculcate a culture of political tolerance before the election.

Exco chair Saleem Mowzer said the council would study the recommendations and findings carefully.

The report would also be sent to the National Intelligence Agency, the Attorney-General's office and the provincial minister for community safety.

Conflict rooted in the past – page 5

CROSSROADS CONFLICT

'Warlords' arm for '99 election

WEAPONS ARE being stockpiled and 'warlords' are planning a comeback in time for next year's polls in one of South Africa's most famous shacklands — Crossroads. **WILLEM STEENKAMP** and **CHRIS BATEMAN** report.

THE city council yesterday moved to address 20 years' worth of internecine violence and power struggles in Crossroads and Philippi that have blocked housing and service delivery. The council warned of an arms build-up and simmering conflicts that threaten to disrupt voting in these areas next year.

A hard-hitting report released yesterday by the City of Cape Town details how the tangled political and social fabric of Crossroads and Philippi is evolving, pitting anti-development traditionalists — who fear losing their vice-like financial and political grip on these communities — against new-era pro-development democrats.

The city also says it has heard evidence that a "third force" aligned to the former grouping is stockpiling arms in preparation for fresh conflict.

City manager and local electoral officer Andrew Boraine said yesterday he was "concerned" about the trend in Crossroads. The council would debate the report at its next meeting in January, but he called for "some sort of summit" of all political parties in the immediate future to commit to a code of conduct promoting political tolerance.

The report, the result of six months of investigation by a commission of inquiry headed by human rights lawyer and presently acting judge Essa Moosa, Independent Mediation Service of SA panelist Geraldine Coy and religious leader Mlamli Mfenyana, was presented to the council at its final 1998 monthly meeting, held yesterday.

The commission was initiated at a cost of about R300 000 earlier this year after a Crossroads grouping, the Women's Power Group (WPG), occupied the Nyanga Crossroads municipal offices in January to protest against the lack of housing and services, payment of service charge arrears and the conduct of officials.

The report found that the primary cause of violence in Crossroads and Philippi was "political intolerance" between parties, organisations and individuals. "These differences were exploited by criminal elements which exacerbated the situation."

It pointed specifically to traditionalist leaders or "warlords" trying to "make a comeback". They included Johnson Ngxobongwana (a former Crossroads leader and leader of the state-sponsored "*witdoeke*" vigilantes, now a New National Party MPP), his former bitter rival but present ally Jeffrey Nongwe (a Crossroads squatter leader who, after being a member of the ANC, is now a PAC member), and Philippi squatter leader Christopher Toise (now in prison facing two charges of attempted murder).

The commission found evidence that they, the Western Cape United Squatters' Association, disaffected ANC members and the United Democratic Movement hijacked the WPG's cause to further their aims.

This group was pitted against the pro-development grouping of the ANC — specifically councillors Depoutch Elese, Melford Gwayi and Sidney Ncate — and the SA National Civics Organisation (Sanco).

Evidence was that a third force of "criminal elements" drawn from former liberation armies such as MK and Apla, as well as self-defence units, was fomenting violence and "stockpiling arms which could be used to win turf in Crossroads on the eve of the forthcoming elections and to disrupt ... the run-up to the elections".

The report placed ultimate blame on all the political parties and civic bodies for the intolerance in the area.

The report found that claims of involvement by Pagad and the radical Muslim grouping Qibla in assisting the WPG were inconclusive.

Other findings included:

- ANC councillors Ncate, Gwayi and Elese were remiss in addressing the grievances of the community.
- The three have been associated with perpetrators of violence, such as alleged taxi-war hitman Victor Sam, which was "untenable and against public policy", though the commission found no evidence of their direct involvement in violence.
- No evidence of nepotism by Elese on the appointment of people to work at a Tupperware factory adjacent to Crossroads, nor evidence of the councillors being involved in the election of members of the local RDP forum — but that Elese and Gwayi being involved in the appointment of a crèche principal was unacceptable.
- No proof of corruption against the three was found regarding allegations about the awarding of tenders and allocation of sites.
- The councillors failed to be accountable to the community — in some cases holding themselves accountable only to their own supporters — and did not co-operate with community-based structures. This

❐ Turn to Page 3

'Warlords' arm for polls

❑ From Page 1

may have contributed to the potential for violence.

"The commission gained the impression that these councillors felt threatened in that their authority, as public representatives, was being undermined by these 'structures'," said the report, adding that the councillors "did not accept criticism" from the public.

● The commission also found evidence of strife within the ANC regarding conflict between the Buntubakhe branch of the ANC in Unathi, Crossroads, and Elese.

● Area police, commanded by Simon Mpembe, didn't have enough manpower and the community did not trust them.

However, Mpembe's bid to improve the police service was "to be highly commended" and his attempts to stabilise the situation had produced "positive results".

The effects of the conflict over the past 11 months were that housing and service delivery were stymied, councillors and council officials were attacked and exposed to danger, schooling was disrupted and law enforcement was affected.

Boraine said placing the allocation of scarce resources in a "desperate" area such as Crossroads in independent hands was crucial in addressing the power struggle.

The problem was that without accountable resource allocation, pumping money into a poverty-stricken area merely exacerbated the situation and placed power in the hands of certain individuals.

"The person who can provide land becomes all-powerful," said Boraine.

Moves to launch a special resource allocation body were far advanced, he said.

Report recommendations include training councillors to fulfil their mandates fairly, teaching the community about government and their rights, improving law enforcement, getting political parties to accept responsibility for members' discipline and addressing the socio-economic problems in the area.

METRO NEWS — SUNDAY TIMES METRO March 14 1999 3

The Cape's tinderbox ignites

As police and solidiers flooded into KTC and Nyanga after five political assassinations in one week, BABALWA SHOTA (left) spoke to mourning family members and neighbours and JANET HEARD (right) tried to find out what went wrong

We used to laugh a lot in this house, now a good man is dead

WHEN Zolile Tyandela, an ordinary UDM member, left his KTC home on Monday evening he asked his neighbour Nomzamo Willem to look after the pot of samp he was cooking for his two sons.

But Nkosinathi and Runta Tyandela never got a chance to enjoy the meal with their father — Willem threw out the samp that night when they received news that Tyandela had been shot dead.

This week Willem talked of the man she respectfully called Tat'omkhulu (grandfather).

"He was a very good father and had a wonderful sense of humour. We used to laugh a lot in this house," she said.

"When he came home on Monday he took a bath, then went to buy paraffin for the stove. He cleaned the samp, put it on the stove and asked me to look after it while he went to see a friend. His pots are still here," she said, pointing at three shiny pots piled on top of a paraffin stove.

When Tyandela, a street sweeper who worked for the council, had not returned home by 10pm, his son Nkosinathi went to look for him.

Willem said that when he came back Nkosinathi was crying and shouting that his father was dead.

"He was a strong and quiet man. He worked hard for the council and did not drink. He liked to stay home and drink his tea. I don't know why he had to leave the house that day," said Willem as she struggled to hold back the tears.

Willem said Tyandela was proud of his backyard garden where he grew mealies.

She said: "Every evening after work, no matter how tired he was, he would water the garden. He also tried to make the front yard look pretty by planting colourful flowers. He was a homemaker who liked nature."

Tyandela's wife and three daughters are at the family's Transkei home, where he is to be buried next Saturday. His sons are staying with an uncle in New Cross Roads until they leave for the Transkei on Friday.

The KTC homes of slain UDM vice-chairman Ntsikana Ngqwata were both deserted this week. In Nyanga, no one knew where to find the family of the party's chairman, Baba Dyonase, who was killed along with Tyandela.

READY FOR ACTION: Soldiers patrol the KTC informal settlement on Friday in the wake of political violence in the area — Picture: RICHARD SHOREY

Dedicated to his community — and senselessly slain

ANC ward councillor Zwelinzima Hlazo, 44, who was shot dead in Nyanga last Sunday evening, had dedicated his life to serving his community and his family.

He was a good man and father, said his eldest brother, Victor, who did not know how the family would survive without Hlazo.

"He believed strongly in education and sport and was financially supporting a soccer club back home in the Transkei.

"When he was not busy with his work, you would find him playing soccer with the young boys. Wherever he went, he searched for young people so he could discuss sport and education," said Victor, 57, who added that his brother was an honest man who was popular with the community.

Local ANC chairman Vuyisile Reshe said: "Zwelinzima was a hard worker who never had a grievance against anyone. When he was attacked he was coming home from voter registration education. It is not just this ward that has lost a good man, but the whole of Nyanga."

Hlazo's 15-year-old son, Masibulele, said he was worried about the family's future now that his father was dead. "My mother does not work and my other relatives are struggling. I don't know who is going to pay for our education."

Reshe said the killings in the Nyanga-KTC area were puzzling as he he did not know of any conflict between the UDM and the ANC.

"As the chairman of the ANC, I would know if there was trouble between the parties, but there is none. We meet and discuss issues that affect the community, but otherwise we stay away from each other. The UDM people were one of us (ANC) before changing parties."

● Seven ANC members appeared in the Mitchells Plain magistrate's court charged with the murder of UDM leader Vulindlela Matiyase at Samora Machel in Philippi.

Their bail application was postponed to March 29 and they were remanded in custody. Some of them also face charges of fraud.

Four UDM members also appeared in the magistrate's court charged with attempted murder, intimidation and fraud.

Police are investigating murder and corruption allegations against the UDM members.

Their bail applications were postponed till tomorrow.

Political parties and police woke up too late

A MEDIATOR investigating conflict in the Philippi-Crossroads areas said it was "earth-shattering" that political parties, civic authorities and the police did not react sooner to a four-month-old warning that violence was imminent in the area.

Five people died this week in politically related violence in Nyanga and another person was killed six weeks ago in Philippi.

Geraldine Coy, one of the three people commissioned by the Cape Town City Council to write a report on tensions in Philippi-Crossroads, said recommendations in the report — such as stepped-up police investigations into the stockpiling of weapons — had not been fully acted upon.

Four months ago, Coy, a professional mediator, recommended a meeting between all players aimed at setting up a code to prevent violence in the wake of rising tension and an alarming build-up of arms in the townships.

Last week local election officer Andrew Boraine, who is also Cape Town city manager, met intelligence and police officers to discuss emergency plans for the elections.

Boraine also took the 323-page Crossroads-Philippi report to a meeting of the multi-party liaison committee, which encompasses all parties, including the ANC and UDM.

They spoke about the stockpiling of weapons and the importance of ensuring political tolerance. Officials agreed to meet next Thursday to plan a meeting to ensure political tolerance and to set up a code of conduct.

But before the second meeting could take place ANC councillor Zwelinzamo Hlazo and UDM member Mncedisi Mpongwana were shot dead. The following day the UDM's Nyanga chairman, Baba Dyonase, and UDM member Zolile Tyandela were killed. The next day the UDM's KTC vice-chairman, Ntsikane Ngqwata, was shot dead.

The deaths followed the January 24 assassination of UDM member Vulindlela Matyase at Samora Machel — a new and heavily contested housing area in Philippi — the day after KwaZulu-Natal UDM leader Sifiso Nkabinde was murdered.

In September 1997 Johnson Mbewana, who reportedly had links with the ANC and the National Consultative Forum — which later became the UDM — was killed in KTC.

Coy said she was "disappointed, but not surprised" that this week's assassinations had taken place. "We had the opportunity at the time to build responsible electioneering campaigning strategies and we missed the boat."

It was not too late, however, to establish all-party pre-election guidelines.

Describing the Western Cape as a "tinderbox", Coy said it was up to all the players — the police, political parties and local authorities — to establish strong election guidelines and to restore peace.

"If a code of conduct was in place, political parties would then have to take responsibility and discipline their members for stepping out of line. Without this, we will continue to have protective responses, justification and blame instead of parties taking responsibility."

A STRUGGLE FOR TERRITORY

THE violence in Nyanga and KTC goes far deeper than political rivalry in the run-up to elections, analysts and mediators said this week.

Rivalry between the new kid on the block — the UDM — and the ANC could be identified as the immediate cause of the killings, but beneath the surface lies a deep-seated struggle for control of housing and transport. Adding fuel to the fire is a historic breakdown in civic authority.

Geraldine Coy, who has spent months assessing the causes of conflict in the Philippi-Crossroads area, said there was a constant realignment of political allegiances, with people switching parties for opportunistic reasons.

These could include the provision of housing sites and the conflict in the taxi industry.

"There are people who are notably fickle. If a person wants to further his territorial interests with warfare, he will do it with the party best able to do that."

The Legal Resources Centre's Kobus Pienaar said the "appalling socio-economic conditions" — such as acute lack of space and housing — opened the door wide for "warlordism, fierce competition and a total breakdown of structures". There was an urgent need for the rapid provision of land to ease the pressure.

Sean Tate, of the Urban and Monitoring Awareness Group, said the conflict stemmed from a complex range of issues: the allocation and scarcity of housing and land — leading to territorial battles — the rift in the community on issues of impartiality concerning the police and the Community Policing Forum, taxi wars and the growing tension between UDM and ANC supporters in the run-up to the elections.

He said there had been reports of intimidation and increasing antagonism between the two parties.

"These issues have come together and have sparked, because of the dry wood lying around."

As this was an ANC stronghold there was extra tension. "The two parties are now vying for the same support, as the UDM tries to gain a foothold in the area," said Pienaar. He hoped the violence would be contained with the deployment of police and with initiatives such as yesterday's all-party summit.

INTERNATIONAL **profile**

HR with a dangerous edge in South Africa

Making and implementing unpopular decisions might be just another part of the job for some HR professionals but for South African Geraldine Coy simply doing her job has brought death threats. BY TRACEY EVANS

When she began to receive phone calls and messages, threatening her life and the lives of her husband and two children, Geraldine Coy knew it was time to leave her country.

Due to arrive in Australia this month to begin a new life, Coy is angry yet philosophical about her self-imposed exile.

"I do feel resentful because it's not a decision that was made for the right reasons. It's a decision that was made because of circumstances beyond my control, and I'm angry with that. Basically what I've lost is a very successful consultancy, I live in a beautiful part of the world and my life has changed overnight."

It was her role as one of three members of a commission of inquiry into township violence that led to the threats on her life. The commission's hard-hitting report, handed down late last year after six months of investigation, named individuals and groups responsible for the violence and made recommendations.

The inquiry was initiated by Cape Town City Council to consider solutions to the 20 years of violence and corruption in Crossroads and Philippi. Murders and assaults are common and the power struggles between warring traditional groups have stymied new housing developments and the delivery of other services.

Coy was left with the task of drafting the Commission's report, placing her in the front line for attacks, after the head of the commission, human rights lawyer Essa Moosa, was appointed an acting judge and was unavailable. The third commissioner, religious leader Mlamli Mfenyana, lives in the community and according to Coy, could not have been expected to take sides.

"When I drafted the report I had to make a judgment call. I knew that what I wanted to say was going to very dangerous and controversial, but I believed that if I didn't say what needed to be said, then the trust that had been invested in me by the people who talked to me so openly would be destroyed. They wanted to get something done about the violence.

"So I felt I had to make a choice. I discussed it with my family and we agreed that I should go ahead and take whatever came."

Despite the upheaval it has caused in her life and the constant fear for the safety of her children, Coy says she would make the same choice again today "because it was the honest thing to do".

The move to mediation

Coy's appointment to the commission of inquiry came about because of her reputation as a mediator. As a consultant, working with Gouws Woods and Partners since 1989 and later as a partner in the Achievement Network Africa, she has helped to break deadlocks between community groups and to settle disputes between unions and management in both private and public sector organisations. Coy is also a panellist for the Independent Mediation Services of South Africa and a member of the Commission for Conciliation, Mediation and Arbitration.

She believes one of the keys to a successful mediation is in achieving the "conditional trust" of all parties involved. "In approaching the process, they'll be feeling vulnerable, not really knowing where they're going to come out and knowing there are going to have to be compromises made, but not sure to what extent those compromises are going to affect them. So conditional trust is important."

The credibility of the mediator is also crucial as well as a willingness by the parties to find a solution.

Coy says of the more than 400 mediations she has facilitated in the past seven years, only two have failed. "I'm not saying that's because I'm a fantastic mediator. It's because mediation is about the parties themselves. The mediator's role is to simply expose the parties to the options in such a way as to make settlement possible, without either party feeling like they've been run over by a truck."

"Some mediators are more successful at that than others. You need to put in the hard work. You wouldn't, for example, dream of closing a mediation at 5 o'clock in the afternoon, because the parties wanted to go home, if there was a chance that they might settle it that evening. You've got to be sensitive to the timeframes and the dynamics between them to know whether it's appropriate to take a break, and usually isn't because it means the parties can 'escape' from the heat of the process. It allows them to re-group and then you lose the energy," says Coy.

Beginning a mediation can sometimes be a tricky task as the often hostile parties stare each other down across the table.

Coy recommends an immediate attempt at disfusing the tension by explaining the way the mediation will work.

"We begin by deliberately avoiding what is on the table, the subject the parties are ▸

INTERNATIONAL PROFILE

Despite the upheaval it has caused in her life and the constant fear for the safety of her children, Coy says she would make the same choice again today "because it was the honest thing to do".

◀ fighting about. We talk about process, what the parties' relationship had been in the past, how they had worked together and what got them to this point. We talk around the issue.

"Then we ask each of the parties to give their perspective on the issue without allowing the other party to interrupt. We don't allow them to address each other directly across the table at that point. We tell them that for our own reference we need to get a perspective on what their needs are. The other party may ask questions of clarification only. That in itself prevents them from taking up positions with each other.

"Next we separate the parties, with their permission, and work with each in different rooms. This is particularly important the more sensitive the issue is. So, we end up in a period of shuttle diplomacy, moving from one room to another. What happens in that process is what we call 're-framing'."

Coy says this is a useful technique for finding the real meaning and issues behind the confrontational language that is often used by parties in dispute.

She says that in the workplace, one of the most common reasons for disputes is an intransigent management style and in South Africa, that is compounded by an increasingly empowered workforce. "And the two inevitably must clash and then it becomes a battle of principles. You start hearing statements like: 'It is my right'; 'It is a principle that cannot be broken'; or, 'It is a precedent that must be set'. In other words the parties are saying: 'I am now drawing the line and you must not cross that line'."

Managing change

Coy's other significant career focus has been change management, an area in which, as a young graduate, she received a baptism of fire.

Having spent her first year in the workforce as an international windsurfing instructor ("a bit of a joke, because in Johannesburg we were a long way from the water – the only thing we had were a few small lakes and very little wind at all"), in 1983 Coy was hired as a personnel officer at Trident Steel, a steel manufacturer employing more than 2,000 people. Trident is part of the Anglo Vaal group of companies.

Within six months she had been promoted to human resources manager and handed the task of desegregating the workplace and ensuring equal opportunity for both black employees and women.

"There were no women or blacks in managerial positions at all, those jobs were reserved for white males only. White women worked as support staff only, the only black women in the organisation were cleaners and the engineering jobs, such as truck and crane drivers, were all held by men. It was a very stereotypical environment. There was job reservation for white men in supervisory positions, so the highest paid black male employees were crane drivers.

"Changing all of that that involved both changing the gender distribution as well as changing racial groupings," she says.

There were also practical issues to worry about such as the use of toilets. White employees had access to clean inside toilets while black employees were expected to use "absolutely disgusting" outside toilets.

At the time the international sanctions against South Africa's apartheid regime were just underway and Anglo Vaal subscribed to the Sullivan Code, a voluntary code of practice that imposed requirements for social responsibility and non-discriminatory behaviour on companies doing business in South Africa.

While change was in the air, many struggled to hold onto the old ways. "There was enormous pressure both inside and outside of the company to maintain the status quo.

More threats

In this position too, Coy received death threats as both blacks and women began to move into the management ranks although, she says, she did not take the threats seriously.

In the six years Coy was employed by Trident, she completed the massive task set for her as a 23-year-old graduate, and moved on to the consultancy, Gouws Woods and Partners, firstly as a consultant and later as a partner. While she worked on projects requiring skills in many different areas including HR management, industrial relations, training and mediation, the lessons she learned at Trident about managing change ensured that it has remained a focus of her career.

Coy says the first and most important part of any change is education. "You don't go into a change program without educating and consulting all employees. I call it 'scoping the organisation'. It's important that you don't make assumptions about the issues. You need to assess the culture of the organisation first, so that at least you know where you are.

"Then you need to decide, as objectively as possible, where you need to be and you do that by asking people to walk with you through that process, that's part of the education process.

Coy says that another important task in managing change is to ensure that you deal with people's anxieties and the threats they perceive. "You need to work out ways of managing the change process with them in a way that doesn't threaten them. Obviously there comes a time when the line has to be drawn but that would only be as a last resort," she says.

Coy says it is surprisingly common for organisations implementing change to forget the people involved.

"One of the best examples is in business process re-engineering. An organisation will say: 'We know what the efficiencies should be, given the nature of the technology and the innovation we have, but this is what we're currently getting, therefore our people are useless'. Then they believe the solution is to push their employees harder, realign them and put down their work processes in a more logical way. But they do all of this without actually talking to the employees and bringing them into the process. They don't give the employees the opportunity to have any input and so to implement decisions that are theirs.

"So the biggest mistake is running a change process independently of the people and then expecting them just to fall into roles which they haven't received training for and have no knowledge or understanding of."

Coy points out that once an organisation has decided to consult its employees about change, it must also go into the process with an open mind. She says she often sees management paying lip service to consultation while all the time having its own agenda.

"Very often managers do espouse all these great philosophies, but when push comes to shove what they're really saying is: 'Yes I'll do it because I think I might look good, but only when the outcome doesn't really matter to me. When it does really matter, I'm going to retain my power'.

"That's when the organisation must change the way it thinks before it begins the process of change, otherwise it could be damaging. In other words, I would recommend that an organisation do nothing until it is truly ready to begin to embrace the change process.

Last year Coy co-founded The Achievement Network Africa, a franchise operation and consultancy and part of the international organisation The Achievement Network. The challenge of establishing a new business is one of the things Coy says she's sad to leave behind as she heads to Australia. In 12 months the business had expanded to four partners and 17 accredited program users.

Nonetheless, aside from the upheavals of moving family and possessions and finding new work, Coy says at least she has the windsurfing to look forward to. Her "dinosaur" windsurfer ("it's one of the original ones") has been carefully packed and she is looking forward to trying it out on Australian waters. ■

PHOTOGRAPHY: ANDREW BROWN

ABOUT THE AUTHOR – GERALDINE COY

Geraldine Coy is the international author of Brave Truth, an accomplished corporate senior manager, a business owner, a diversity and community worker, a leadership and personal development coach, an agent for positive change and a mother.

One of six children, Geraldine was schooled in South Africa and England. As a child she was very physically active, competing in the State diving team and later gaining an international windsurfing instructor's license.

Growing up in South Africa during a time of turmoil and tension ignited Geraldine's passion for racial and gender equality and respect. She studied Clinical Psychology and English at university before becoming the first female manager in the steel industry in South Africa when she took up the position of Personnel Manager for Trident Steel – a company with more than 2000 employees.

In a cultural setting that precluded black South Africans from aspiring to skilled and semi-skilled jobs, Geraldine made significant positive change by creating a program that brought these employees into management positions.

In 1984, Geraldine married and in the next few years had her first two children. She joined a consulting company in Cape Town and was offered a partnership within six months before moving on to work in the management development field to prepare communities for the transition to a democratic South Africa.

Geraldine's skills as a mediator, a human resource specialist, a protector of human rights and a promoter of peace and equality were in high demand in the years that followed. She was involved in many important ways towards the end of the apartheid movement and in establishing a democratic South Africa.

While juggling family demands and the arrival of her third child, Geraldine's involvement in formulating public policy, participating in the running of the 1994 election, mediating community and industrial disputes and her role on the National Peace Secretariat, all led up to her role in a commission of enquiry that published a report of findings into violent atrocities committed in two of Cape Town's townships.

After this report was published, Geraldine received threats against her family that resulted in the family relocating to Australia for the safety of her children.

Relocating was a difficult time but Geraldine's skills were soon in demand in a new senior national managerial role at Telstra.

This was the beginning of her career in Australia. She was subsequently headhunted by Bakers Delight to become their General Manager of Organisational Effectiveness, before moving on to Executive Director of Human Resources and Change Management for WorkSafe Victoria and other senior corporate roles.

Now the owner of the highly successful Red Tin Shed – an executive coaching business, Geraldine is helping others to achieve their professional and personal goals as well as continuing to pursue her own goals of creating positive change in communities.

Geraldine has worked and travelled extensively throughout Africa, UK, Europe, South East Asia, Mexico, North and South America and New Zealand.

She holds many professional memberships and affiliations, including being a member of several professional and executive coaching associations, the Cranlana Colloquium and the International Society for Coaching Psychology.

Geraldine lives in Melbourne with her husband, David and youngest daughter, Rachel.

RESOURCES

Listing of Acronyms

ANC	African National Congress
APLA	Azanian Peoples Liberation Army (Armed wing of the PAC)
CCMA	Commission for Conciliation, Mediation and Arbitration
COSATU	Congress of South African Trade Unions
CRORA	Crossroads Residents Association
IDASA	Institute for a Democratic Alternative for South Africa
IFP	Inkatha Freedom Party
IMSSA	Independent Mediation Services of South Africa
IRISA	Industrial Relations Institute of South Africa
ISLP	Integrated Serviced Land Project
NP	National Party
PAC	Pan Africanist Party
PAGAD	People Against Gangsters and Drugs

PAWC	Provincial Administration of the Western Cape
RDP	Reconstruction and Development Programme
SAAF	South African Air Force
SANCO	South African National Civics Association
SANDF	South African National Defence Force
WECUSA	Western Cape United Squatters Association
WITS	The University of the Witwatersrand

Recommended Reading

- Long Walk to Freedom – The autobiography of Nelson Mandela
- Mandela – The Authorised Portrait – Foreword by Kofi Annan, past Secretary-General, United Nations
- A new illustrated history of South Africa – ed Trewhella Cameron, advisory ed S.B Spies
- Voices from Robben Island – compiled and photographed by Jurgen Schadeberg
- UBUNTU – The Spirit of African Transformation Management – Lovemore Mbigi with Jenny Maree
- Re-thinking Popular justice – self-regulation and civil society in South Africa – Daniel Nina
- Reader's Digest Illustrated History of South Africa – the real story – Expanded third edition.
- South Africa 1990 – 1994 – The Miracle of a Freed Nation – Sunday Times edition
- Tomorrow is Another Country – Allister Sparks
- Beyond the Miracle – Inside the New South Africa – Allister Sparks
- Every Secret Thing – my family my country – Gillian Slovo
- Tutu Voice of the Voiceless – Shirley du Boulay

- Pale Native – Memories of a renegade reporter – Max du Preez
- Diary of an Exile – Steve Jacobs
- F W de Klerk – The Autobiography – The Last Trek A New Beginning
- Ink in the Porridge – Urban Legends of the South African elections – Arthur Goldstuck

Reference Notes

1. **Ruda Landman** was a television journalist/interviewer.

2. **Homelands** – These were tracts of land identified by the apartheid government which were set aside for the confinement of black people, who were registered as resident there, and only allowed a temporary "Pass" of 72 hours at any time to visit relatives. If caught outside the curfew, people were arrested, detained and regularly forced to pay fines for release. The homelands represented about 13 (thirteen) per cent of South Africa, into which 75 (seventy five) per cent of the population was confined. The homelands were loosely situated on tribal "homelands of origin", although the more arable and viable land was set aside for the white farming community. The homelands were therefore hardly financially viable as the lands could not sustain the population, forcing a transient labour system. For example, men were given a twelve month working pass to work on the mines in and around Johannesburg, where they were accommodated in hostels, leaving their families behind in the homelands. Much has been written of the terrible conflicts between men of different tribal origins within these hostels. A closer examination of social interaction would have a deeper read again of the real drivers of much of the conflict, often associated with the availability and movement of a transient supply of women who distributed favours, causing disassociation and disenfranchised communities all over South Africa.

   Some homelands, because there were intermittently good pieces of land of value, were split up into a number of different locations, (like Bophutatswana) , making them politically as well as financially unviable. Homeland leaders were hardly recognised as players in

South Africa's future, the only real exception at this level, being Chief Mangosutho Buthelezi, Chief of the Zulu nation of Kwa-Zulu.

The Transkei, enjoined as it was to the Ciskei, was the most viable and independent homeland of the time.

3. **The Wiehahn Commission** , was a consequence of the recommendations of the earlier Riekert Commission of the South African government, which focussed on the need to build productivity in organisations in the early 1970's. The recommendations of this commission led to some of the most significant historical changes to the legislation in apartheid South Africa. These included;

    - Legal recognition of Black Trade Unions.
    - Abolition of statutory job reservation.
    - Retention of the closed shop bargaining system.
    - The creation of the National Manpower Commission, and
    - The introduction of the Industrial Court to resolve industrial litigation.

    (Ref. South Africa History Online)

4. **Section 10 (1) (d)** of the Group Areas legislation – allowed for twelve month working passes to be granted to black people seeking work. The idea was that these people would return to the homelands every twelve months for their annual leave of 2/3 weeks, and so earn the right for a renewal of a temporary pass. This is the reference to "Pass" which will be found in the book.

5. **Umkhonto we Sizwe** (abbreviated as **MK**, translated as "**Spear of the Nation**") was the armed wing of the African National Congress (ANC), co-founded by Nelson Mandela, which fought against the South African government. MK launched its first guerrilla attacks against government installations on 16 December 1961. It was subsequently classified as a terrorist organisation by the South African government and the United States, and banned.

   For a time it was headquartered in Rivonia, a suburb of Johannesburg. On 11 July 1963, 19 ANC and MK leaders, including Arthur Goldreich and Walter Sisulu, were arrested at Liliesleaf Farm, Rivonia). The farm was privately owned by Arthur Goldreich and bought with South African Communist Party and ANC funds, as individuals who were not deemed "White" were unable to own such a property under the Group Areas Act. This was followed by the Rivonia Trial, in which ten leaders of the ANC were tried for 221 acts of sabotage designed to "foment violent revolution". Wilton Mkwayi, chief of MK at the time, escaped during trial.

   MK was integrated into the South African National Defence Force by 1994. - Source definition Wikipedia

BRAVE TRUTH The Board Game®

Background & History

The board game is a creation from author, speaker and corporate change expert Geraldine Coy. Following on from her book "Brave Truth" the board game is a real life example of how to benefit from the power of truth and the trust it brings from others, when the truth is told.

The game has been adapted from a similar game called "Interlink" that was made In the mid 1980's, and developed in South Africa, to prepare youth groups for an emerging new South Africa, post apartheid. Nelson Mandela was released in 1990, and was inaugurated as State President in 1994, so Interlink was developed inside the apartheid regime. Ric Matthews from Interlink, used the board game as a method of engaging youth groups in discussion, where before this would have been very difficult. The game formed the central activity for youth groups (year 12 school leavers at that time), over a five day residential course. The groups were comprised of twenty four 17 – 18 year old adolescents from multi racial, multi cultural, multi socioeconomic groupings.

Brave Truth The Board Game® is designed for our present time, and appropriate for groups and organisations who are looking at transformation within their ranks, generating deep and enhanced appreciation for the richness of our diverse community. As a cross-cultural initiative, this board game will raise awareness and sensitivity to racism, sexism, gender bias, sexual preference, religious affiliation, family values, socio-economic, and political experience. Players will experience a significant shift in their world views in their experience of this game. Brave Truth The Board Game® has been designed with built in flexibility for application in youth groups and at the boardroom table. Specific issues can be built into the framework on a tailored basis. Brave Truth promotes mutual co-operation and builds trust in groups who play the game. Individuals walk away with improved confidence in their own worth and that of their colleagues.

Principles

The objective of the programme is to develop and enrich relationships by encouraging people to express their specific personal views, and to discover and respect the views and values of other cultural groups. A lasting and creative foundation is laid for future co-operation and understanding between groups. This platform allows for future interaction to take place in a constructive and supported environment by building leadership within the communities who will continue to mentor both the outcomes, and new recruits undergoing the change process.

The course is designed to ensure that there is maximum participation from all individuals, but allows for personal determination of the level of vulnerability, (thus reducing resistance and maximising openness to new ideas and learning). Without exception in practice, even the most reserved individuals have engaged and grown in confidence of their own worth. Ongoing communication enables individuals to deal with conflict creatively, and to learn the value of mutual interdependence and a commitment to build a resilient community.

Course Content

- Management of preconceptions.

The participants undergo an experiential discovery of subconscious beliefs, personal perceptual frameworks, including natural preconceptions. They learn how to recognise these, and to manage them.

- Development of meaningful relationships.

Extensive and carefully facilitated interaction is generated within a maximum of 4 teams of 6 people. By means of the board game, participants share information about themselves, and to each other, in a non-judgmental and confidential manner, which ensures that their relationships are cemented through a growth in understanding of similarities, rather than a focus on their differences. Cross – cultural understanding is progressively developed, and trust is an established consequence. Questions on What? Why? How? Are answered in a progressively enhanced (deeper) way as the programme progresses.

Outcomes

Trust between cultural groupings, certainly between the participants is a key outcome. The programme is most effective with initiation through community/youth leadership, or organisational leadership, and then followed up by participation from other members of their communities or from the organisation, in like diversity of groupings This allows for the building up of a critical mass to support real change within the communities/organisations.

To demonstrate this, each group is set a task to fulfil by the facilitators, which would previously not have been contemplated before by the diverse groups themselves which they achieve through the benefit of co-operation. This cements the learning and builds confidence in the strengths of their own value within their community or organisation.

Re-entry and follow-up

In order to enhance this, there is a re-entry support for the programme participants. Emphasis is placed on maximising individual learning and relationship building for the benefit of the community as a whole, so that when participants leave the five day programme, they are equipped with a joint plan of action agreed at the workshop. They have identified future possibilities for cross-cultural communication and engagement opportunities. Each team has met with the course facilitators, (and adult leadership members within their community or organisation), to consolidate their proposals for change within the community or organisation.

Post course follow up with the facilitators within two weeks, and thereafter one month from the workshops, ensures that they feel supported by both the facilitators and their own leadership structures, to hold to their agreements. Simultaneously, others begin filtering through the programme, which strengthens the platform.

This programme has a tested platform of success in South Africa, and offers real opportunity in the Australian context against extremism. It is supportive, non-judgemental and develops real tolerance, understanding and self management, which are all great life skills in the management of conflict.